Acting In Faith

A Christian's Guide to the Acting World

MICHAEL KARY

Theopneustos Publishing

Published by Theopneustos Publishing (USA)

First Printing 2016

ISBN 9781682736340

Printed in the United States of America
Designed by Jonathan Marshall

To Karin, my biggest fan and a true Proverbs 31 woman.

Aunt Melva,
　　Mom thought you'd like one of these. If there isn't room on your shelf, maybe you've got a table that needs propping up ☺

Love You!
Michael Kay

Contents

Inspiration

Work Ethic

The Line: Strangers in a Strange Land

The Cost

The Actor's Toolbox

Appendix

End Notes

Preface

Most acting books are a tool, or a means to an end, and that end is either artistic or financial success in a devastatingly difficult career. This is not one of those books. The techniques I write about and the inspiration behind them *can* make you a better actor; the practice may even lead you to some monetary reward, but neither result should be considered an "end". There was a certain amount of trepidation with which I approached the writing of this book. At first, my fears were mostly egocentric (and as an actor, I'm not sure those fears are gone as much as they have moved "upstage"). As I grew closer to putting my beliefs on paper, I was less worried others wouldn't get them or like them, and more worried they would somehow misuse them.

The writing of this book chronicles the discoveries I have made over the first few decades of my career as an actor, and it forms the bridge between that period of my life and my current calling as an acting teacher. I have found plenty of methods, books, and curriculum from which to teach the fundamentals of acting, but the challenges for me in the classroom lay not in the nuts and bolts of performance, but in the "why" of it. Successful students are not satisfied with simple step-by-step processes. They want to get past the "how" because the "why" is where things stick; the "why" is where things get personal, and the personal also happens to be where the best acting happens.

In my own journey, I found there to be a great link between spontaneous, compelling performance and a disciplined study of a proscribed technique. Whether the person has studied Stanislavski, Meisner, Chekhov, Suzuki, or any combination of them, the disciple of these techniques is bound to turn in something worth watching. However, I have also seen beginners, from children to adults, achieve moments of inspired transcendence on stage and on camera. Technique was important, but there was something else behind it. What was it? How did it work? Was it available to anyone? Whenever I have encountered questions like these in other areas of my life, I would seek counsel. On matters of greater importance, I would invariably be led back to God and His Word. The same was true here.

The more I studied acting, and the more I probed the Bible, the more I saw Biblical themes popping out of the major acting techniques and methodologies. There was no mention of God, but His fingerprints were everywhere. The great acting teachers spoke of the art form with a religious reverence. For example, Stanislavski (whose immediate audience was a communist and strictly atheistic society), even went so far as to call theatre, "...a pulpit, which is the most powerful means of influence." He also described actors as, "...priest(s) of beauty and truth." (Moore pg. 3) Stella Adler said, "The theatre is a spiritual and social X-ray of its time. The theatre was created to tell people the truth about life and the social situation." Larry Moss adds this, "That's what our work (acting) can do: we remind people that things can change, that wounds can heal, that people can be forgiven, and that closed hearts can open again." These great men and women of the theatre recognized a connection between performance and an outside, dare I say spiritual, influence. In much the same way the apostle Paul recognized the spiritualism of the Greeks and gave an identity to an unnamed god, I hope to assign a place for the truths we find in the great acting techniques of the world.

I began making the connections between God and my work with a study in the book of Philippians. Philippians 2:3-4 talks about having a reason for everything you do, and making sure you put the needs of others before yourself. To me, that spoke directly to the proper way of employing tactics in a scene. Being a present and supportive scene partner echoed the Bible's recurring message of, "Loving your neighbor as yourself." Researching given circumstances and stepping into a foreign character's shoes is the equivalent to experiencing empathy with another human being (a key component to sharing the gospel). The parallels between the Bible and the major acting techniques were abundant, and they surprised me. Then I found I was surprised at being surprised. Why shouldn't they pop out? If what the Bible has to say about how to live is true at church, why not in the workplace, at home, and on the stage? Thus, this book was born. In it, we will take the light of the gospel and focus it like a laser beam on how it applies to acting and the entertainment industry. How can we apply the teachings of The Bible to the problems encountered in performance?

The main roadblocks to a successful, engaging performance are the following:

1. Fear
2. Lack of Empathy
3. Absence of Inspiration

The more I learn about God's sovereignty, love and creativity, the more I realize Christian performers have unique solutions to these three key problems. It seems like Christian performers should be the most sought after people in an industry where instead they are looked down on (at best), or avoided (at worst). These three snares should not be the norm for the Christian, but they're as prevalent in Christian performance as they are anywhere else. Why? My theory is that part of the difficulty lies in the overwhelming human desire to compartmentalize. Many of us tend to be one type of person at work, another at home, and perhaps another at church. This tendency is exacerbated when considering the compartmental nature of an actor's job. They are required to assume multiple different identities as a part of their work. The Bible, however, talks of unity: unity with community, unity with ourselves, and unity with Him.

Living a life as a Christian performer can often feel like having a foot in two disparate and warring worlds. One world says your eternity is set in stone, your significance is secure, and your identity is established with Christ. The other world is a mercurial mixture of fame, disappointment, triumph, and ambiguity. We learn from Scripture that "a house divided against itself cannot stand, (Mat 12:25)" and I am positing that this is why many Christian performers fail. They do not know how to navigate both worlds, and as a result their creativity and performances are often divided and fall flat. What makes the difference between a good performance and painful one, and why does Christian drama in particular find itself so often in the "painful" category? Church actors either rely solely on secular methodologies, or shun those methodologies completely. Many muddle through their "skits" with a preconceived notion of what acting should look like or a half-conscious prayer that God will "bless" a performance. Few Christian performers understand that the source of many acting techniques can be shifted from the secular back to the sacred. These precious few realize acting is a craft requiring a great deal of discipline, but they also know the power of God to inspire and lead a person through his or her performance. In short, they have made the connection between the fundamentals of their faith and the fundamentals of their vocation.

Half of what it is to be a Christian is accepting our human brokenness as fact. It is coming to a place where we acknowledge that our self-serving attitudes and desires have tainted every aspect of our lives. The other half is coming to know how our sinfulness is completely trumped through the power, life, and work of Jesus Christ. What falls short in performance, and in all of our "every day" lives, is we acknowledge the endemic presence of sin, but we forget how grace is just as pervasive.

Ephesians 6:12 says,

> "For our struggle is not against flesh and blood, [i.e. poor scripts, bad directors, short rehearsal periods] but against the rulers, against the authorities, against the powers of this dark world and against the spiritual forces of evil in the heavenly realms."

The goals of this book are to guide Christian artists in their path, and to keep their feet firmly planted in the eternal security and love of their Creator, while "suffering the slings and arrows of outrageous fortune." Herein you will find a gentle blend of technique, encouragement, exhortation, and Bible study designed to bring out an inspired performance, free from fear and full of empathy. My hope is that you will discover that God is not a means to your personal artistic success, but the opposite; the more you practice your craft with Him as the "why" behind your technique, the closer you will grow toward the Author of your story, and others will be drawn to His light. This is what happens when the gospel gets on stage.

CHAPTER 1

The Parallels

"I think I love and reverence all arts equally, only putting my own just above the others; because in it I recognize the union and culmination of my own. To me it seems as if when God conceived the world, that was Poetry; He formed it, and that was Sculpture; He colored it, and that was Painting; He peopled it with living beings, and that was the grand, divine, eternal Drama."

– Charlotte Cushman[1]

Part I: Two Houses...

"All the world's a stage,
And all the men and women merely players;
They have their exits and their entrances,
And one man in his time plays many parts,
His acts being seven ages."

– Jaques, As You Like It (Act II.vii)[2]

Shakespeare's words, like all great art, tend to change their meanings over time. A few years ago, what used to be a clever catalogue of the ages of man took on a startling new tone for me. What if all the world *was* a stage, and each of us had a part to play? The question has obviously been around for quite a while. It's echoed in plays like Pirandello's *6 Characters in Search of an Author* or in films like *Stranger than Fiction* or *The Truman Show*. It's a question with multiple answers, each of which spring from whatever worldview the person in question holds. For example, if I didn't think each person was responsible for holding to some sort of (dare I say it?) divine destiny, then all of my actions and thoughts would be mine to determine. I would have no outside source from which to gain a sense of purpose or responsibility. In fact, my only obligation would be to my own survival and happiness. There would be no external consequences for my decisions because I would not be bound by any overarching cosmic law, duty, or gratitude. If, however, I did think humans had a part to play, then there would be quite a few different implications to consider. If all the world was a stage, and we were all somehow players in the telling of a great story, then it follows that there must be an author. As an actor, I would also find comfort in knowing that there was a part written that only I could play. This path of reasoning soon opened up a rich parallel between the Theatre and the Christian faith that enabled me to take both my performance and my spiritual pursuits and put them on the same page. The question remains, however, is there a page large enough to contain them both?

Theatre and religion. Religion and theatre. Today, the two fields are apt to vilify each other. Religion says the entertainment industry is a debauched and indulgent swamp where morals are corrupted and souls are lost. Whereas, the entertainment industry sees religion as an unthinking, judgmental, and hypocritical desert where progress withers before it blooms. There was a time, however, when the two grew in tandem, the one feeding the other in a beautiful symbiotic relationship. Some of the greatest literature, music, and art have poured forth from the land of religion. Looking at both realms, it is easy to see why they worked so well together. Their structure has many of the same, or complementary aspects. Perhaps over time, religion began to grow jealous of the claim on sacredness many people of the theatre made, or the people of the theatre may have begun to scorn religion's attempts at theatricality. The cause of the rift is not my concern. What comes *after* is of more importance. Echoing a concern from Shakespeare's Bottom, "The more the pity some honest neighbours will not make them friends."[3]

I would like to be the "neighbours" to whom he refers. I believe it is in the best interests of both worlds to give their former relationship another shot. Let us look closely and see what parallels can be drawn.

Part II: ...Both Alike in Dignity

7:59 p.m. The last of the guests are ushered to their seats by geriatric men and women with flashlights and clip-on bowties. It has been a long week, and each patron is looking forward to putting it behind them for a while. There are already snatches of related conversations.

"Who's in it?"

"Were they good?"

"Remember when we saw it last time?"

Each eye moves with a practiced nonchalance between wristwatches, friends, and the stage where a red veil separates the eager ticket holders from the world of the play.

"The Earth was formless and void..." [4]

8:01 p.m. The voices dim with the lights in silent agreement. The throng is much more than an audience now. In every sense they are a congregation awaiting creation. In the darkness, imagination asserts its power.

"...and darkness was over the surface of the deep..." [4]

8:02 p.m. To a perceptive few in the back row, a barely audible sound reaches their ears. It is a human voice. It isn't coming from the black expanse where the audience has affixed its attention. Instead, the voice comes from outside the space. The voice carries authority, confidence, and power.

"Ready lights one."

A pause.

"Lights one...go."

"Then God said, 'Let there be light,' and there was light." [4]

From 8:03 onward, the stage is awash in pinks, and blues, and bastard ambers. More voices fill the theatre. This time from the stage, the place of action. Each word creating a world that did not exist a few moments before. A story is played out filled with characters who seem unaware that the food they eat, the birds they hear, the sun they feel, even the words they speak have all been painstakingly planned out for them.

Somewhere, outside of the universe of the play, an author has crafted a reality, a director has decided that this particular story needs to be told tonight, and a stage manager has brought together the resources to make it possible. Tonight, people will fall in love. They will make poor choices and great sacrifices. Some of them will die. Why? Is it for the characters? The audience? The artists? Questions like these can be answered by using theatre as a microcosm for humanity's experience in the cosmos.

How different was the first day of creation to an opening night? Whether a comedy or tragedy, playwrights form realities in which there are characters who either adhere to their new world's statutes and mores, or they do not. The next two hours is spent learning what happens to them. Do they succeed? Do they fail? What are the consequences of each heroic or villainous act?

In classical drama, the world is often set up in its ideal state; it is then upended in some way, until, through a variety of physical, spiritual, or social obstacles it is finally set to rights again. I see little difference between this paradigm and the dramatic through-line of the Bible. We start in the garden; we wander in the desert or in exile. Finally, the Author Himself steps in and sets the world back to its original ideal. The Greeks had a name for this type of conclusion: the *Deus Ex Machina*, the machine of the gods. It is as if they somehow knew humanity would need some outside help at the end of all things.

How different are the playwright, the director, and the stage manager from the Christian doctrine of the trinity? Aside from the obvious answer of human fallibility, these three care for the world of a play or film in much the same way God, in His three persons, cares for His creation.

God the Father, I will argue is the playwright. We are under His rules while we play in His house. If God wants gravity to pull objects together with a force directly proportional to their masses, then humans get the privilege of walking on the ground. If He wants to set a standard of perfection that must be met in order to commune with Him, then anything less than that standard will put humans out of that communion. Likewise, if at any time God wants to suspend or amend His rules, then Jesus and Peter can walk on water, water can change its molecular properties and become wine, and humans can have the free will to accept the gift of grace. The people of the world do not have to like (or even acknowledge) the spiritual and physical laws around them, but their opinions or awareness have no bearing on the law's

existence. The playwright's prerogative is likewise ultimate and absolute. The writer also has an intimate knowledge of his people. Only
he knows where their names come from, where their hurts begin, and
why their cards fall the way they do. There is a beautiful passage in
Revelation 2:17 which says,

> "...To him who overcomes, to him I will give some of the hidden
> manna, and I will give him a white stone, and a new name written
> on the stone which no one knows but he who receives it."[5]

Couple that with the familiar passage in Psalm 139:

> "O Lord, You have searched me and known me. You know when
> I sit down and when I rise up; You understand my thought from
> afar. You scrutinize my path and my lying down, and are intimate-
> ly acquainted with all my ways. Even before there is a word on
> my tongue, behold O Lord, You know it all...For You formed my
> inward parts; You wove me in my mother's womb...My frame was
> not hidden from You, when I was made in secret, and skillfully
> wrought in the depths of the earth; Your eyes have seen my un-
> formed substance; and in your book were all written the days that
> were ordained for me, when as yet there was not one of them."[6]

This passage screams of the kind of comprehensive knowledge
only an author can possess.

The concept of an Author-God just made sense to me, and as a
result, my idea of communion with Him morphed and grew beyond
the breaking of bread and drinking of wine. God wasn't bound into
ritual, He was alive in the actions of us, His characters. I am hesitant
to put this next section down on paper because there are enough directors out there with a God-complex. However, it isn't much of a leap
to connect the director of a play with at least part of Christ's role in
the trinity.

Where a director is (or at least should be) bound to honor the playwright, Jesus made repeated claims to have been sent to do the Father's work, and to glorify the Father while doing it.[7] I can also cite the first chapter of John where we see the Word (the work of humanity's playwright) has become flesh (in the person of Jesus)[8]. The players Shakespeare mentions in the quote at the beginning of this chapter need some direction. The only way to get that direction is if there is a liaison between the writer and the characters: someone who can speak the language of the players, who is also in tune with the heart of the poet. A director who can walk that line, and at the same time get his actors to feel as though their choices are their own is the key to great collaborative art. Directors should also look to Jesus as a model of servant leadership. I will address this later, but Jesus conveyed His message to the disciples through story *and* action. He used common places and characters in parables (stories) to personify concepts the Father deemed essential. He also wasn't above showing those twelve men what He meant through action. This goes way beyond giving an actor line readings. Directors must feel comfortable doing anything they ask their actors to do.

I have also seen directors serve their cast and crews in more tangible ways. It says much to a group of people (especially a group who may not know each other) when their leader steps into their midst and hosts a dinner, says a prayer in a troubled time, or even offers a tissue in an emotional rehearsal. A humble director knows he serves both his cast and the playwright. Actors who see this kind of leadership are eager to follow and fulfill a director's vision. Much like Christ, who needed to bring his followers to a point where they could begin aligning their choices with God's will, a director can do the same with every aspect of his production. This should be the goal of any director: align your actor's choices with that of the playwright. The play is paramount. Too often actors are left to make decisions based on their own will. As a result, there are several discordant stories warring for the audience's attention. A single source for character alignment creates an ensemble, one of the most coveted states of being in the theatre.

Unity is a major theme in the Bible. Shortly before Jesus is arrested, He prays for his disciples to gain unity.[9] In fact, when James and John come to Jesus to negotiate over who gets top billing, they are quickly rebuffed.[10] The last thing a director needs is a celebrity personality to manage.

Lastly, I see a similarity in the element of trust that mature directors need to develop. A good director will have to trust in both the quality of the text, and the competence of his actors because he will not (usually) stay past opening night. After the curtain comes down that first night, the director often hops a flight for the next job. I am reminded of the opening night party before Christ is risen from the dead. Granted, it lasted longer than one night, but we are also talking about a much longer run than your average play. At the end of the "party" Jesus makes a short speech and hops a flight to Heaven so he can, "...prepare a place for you."[11] Are the players then left alone? Not at all. Jesus promises them a helper in John 16, starting in verse 13.

> "But when He, the Spirit of truth, comes, He will guide you
> into all the truth; for He will not speak on His own initiative,
> but whatever He hears, He will speak; and He will disclose to you
> what is to come. He will glorify Me, for He will take of Mine
> and will disclose it to you. All things that the Father has are
> Mine; therefore I said that He takes of Mine and will disclose it
> to you." [12]

Keeping with the analogy, the Spirit of Truth, or the Holy Spirit, would take the place of the stage manager. Arguably the toughest, most thankless job in the business, the stage manager keeps things running on task after the director leaves. They are given authority over everything. They open the house. They call each cue. They bring down the law when the cast or crew steps out of line. They hold the Band-aids, and to most people, they are invisible. I find it interesting that the Holy Spirit is called "The Advocate"[13] a couple of verses earlier. That is one of the stage manager's primary functions. They are the actor's and crew's voice to the authority above them. If anyone has an issue of safety, or what they believe to be unfair treatment, the protocol is to go through stage management to get things right. They are the first people on the job, and the last ones to go home. I've seen stage managers talk down stars after a "diva fit" and cradle chorus members in their arms in times of extreme tragedy. We are all equal in the eyes of our stage mangers. The picture of the Holy Spirit is remarkably complete, and we can take the image even further. Like the last part of John 16, stage managers, "...will tell you what is to come."[14] Each technical moment in a play is whispered over the headsets backstage, so each member of the cast and crew knows precisely when to execute their particular tasks. All of these cues are written in a master prompt book, what some people call the show's "Bible".

There is another component to address in our parallel. The actor. Who is he? Is he us, one of the, "...men and women..." who are "merely players?" To this I say both yes and no. The players should be the arms, legs, and voice of the writer. They carry out his will unquestioningly, and they are subject to his fancies and his grace. The way I read God's sovereignty in the Bible, there is a part written for each of us; however, I also read about how humans abandoned the original script. A play with actors who believe the story is theirs, and theirs alone, becomes tiresome. Such actors rarely work, or if they do, they often aren't invited back. No, somewhere along the way, all of us have gone our own way.[15] The good news is there is someone from the artistic staff willing to show us the way back. The director has come across the table to show us how it's done. Some people will say that Jesus came to show us what God was like. While that may be true, I do not think it is complete. If we look at Jesus' words and ministry, He also came to show us how to be human again. He took the original stage directions (the commandments given on Sinai) and fulfilled them.[16] We will discuss this further, but it is important for us to recognize that Jesus also gives actors an incredible example of fully inhabiting a role.

The structure of a theatrical production (creation, conflict, and resolution) shows only a few of the similarities between a play and the Christian's view of God and the Bible. Like all analogies, the similarities can only go so far. The parallels within the chapter are simply meant as one way to show God's fingerprints on our creative processes. They also form the jumping off point for understanding the problems of empathy, fear, and inspiration.

CHAPTER 2

Empathy

"I think it's impossible to really understand somebody, what they want, what they believe, and not love them the way they love themselves." [1]

– Ender Wiggin, *Ender's Game*

According to the Oxford English Dictionary (an indispensible tool to any actor, see my list of tools in chapter 8, The Actor's Toolbox), empathy is: "...the action of understanding, being aware of, being sensitive to, and vicariously experiencing the feelings, thoughts, and experiences of another of either the past or present without having the feelings, thoughts, and experience fully communicated in an objectively explicit manner".[2] This is the core of what actors do. At the very least, they need to make an audience believe they are, "experiencing the feelings, thoughts and experiences of another."

Empathy for the Audience

The actor is the audience's main conduit into the world of the play. They must walk a tightrope between reality and fiction. This may be sacrilege to some who believe it is an actor's job to be so immersed in the work that there is no recognition of the spectators. The fact is, the audience is there, the camera is there, and they both demand a certain amount of attention and care. Hitting marks, projecting the voice, prop manipulation, and the "mechanics" of performance all require awareness of things that do not exist in the character's paradigm. At the same time, the actor must truly believe he is on the deck of a frigate, or she is really being attacked by wolves. If an actor falls into the trap of excluding all but the writer's words on the page, he runs the risk of turning in a great performance that no one is able to see. By the same token, if the performer lets the audience know that he is "in on the joke", then the audience is catapulted out of the work, and the chance for them to achieve any kind of catharsis is lost. Like I said, it's a tightrope, but it is better to acknowledge the tightrope than to pretend it doesn't exist. Many actors feel like failures because they are not able to get the audience out of their brains. Some of the rest become so self-absorbed in their work they become un-directable and difficult scene partners. The key to this tricky balancing act is empathy for their characters AND their audience. Empathy will help with the mechanics of: "Can I be seen?" but it also helps with the performance questions like: "Am I being true to the environment and circumstances?" We cannot forget acting is an art form that requires an audience. We are in this together, so do not leave your patrons in the figurative dark.

Empathy for the Character

Empathy is also critical for character generation. Understanding a character is no different than understanding a person. The key to experiencing empathy for either of them is a matter of perspective. There are two vantage points from which to view a person: from outside their life and from inside it. If you can manage to change your point of view from what you think *about a character* to what the character *thinks about themselves*, both the lines you speak and the words you hear will carry with it a sense of truth because they will be internally motivated rather than externally layered.

How is empathy for a fictional character achieved? There are many acting techniques that use the term "given circumstances". Given circumstances are the facts of the play and of the character. It is easy to confuse facts with judgment, so try to be as discerning as possible. It is not usually a fact that someone is mean. That person may seem mean to the world around them (a judgment) but the facts are the following: they lost their spouse, they are addicted to alcohol, they have a chemical imbalance, they have been bewitched, or they have low blood sugar and need to eat. These facts are found through the text of the play AND ONLY THROUGH THE TEXT. We find them by looking at what our characters have to say about themselves, and often more telling, what the other characters say about them as well. Stage directions written by the author (not the stage manager) also have value. The empathetic actor will look for clues, such as location (geographic, relation to other people on stage, public, private, etc), time (time of day, century, before or after a major event, etc), history (what just happened, what happened a day ago, a year ago, etc), sensory information (is it cold, hot, light, dark, are they in pain, under the influence, etc) and status (who do they work for or with, how much money or power do they have, etc). Using given circumstances will help build a character internally (3 dimensional) rather than externally (2 dimensional). Put in practice, it looks a bit like this: Paul is a man with extensive theological training. This training involves the memorization of holy books and the precise practice of prescribed rituals. His texts and teachers are very clear that to falter in any of the laws laid out in his religion requires a set of sacrifices. A man has come into Paul's life who claims to follow a prophet recently killed for claiming to be the God and king of Paul's people. This man was also once a follower of the same God Paul worships. Paul lives in the first century. All of these facts would put Paul on a donkey, doing the bidding of the priests of Israel, determined to blot out the Christian uprising that is leading a large portion of his own people astray. These given circumstances account for most of what Paul does for the entire book of Acts. It is also precisely why Paul had to meet God in such dramatic fashion, and it probably had a great deal to do with why God chose Paul to be his voice to the Gentiles. An actor playing Paul will want to use these facts to inform how he will respond to the high priests, or Christ's new followers, or the emperor of the known world. It takes some work, but hopefully it is apparent how important it is to interpret a character in this fashion.

THE ACTOR'S HOMEWORK:

1. Take a character you are currently researching and find at least three facts in the text for each of the following categories:

    a. Who is he in relationship to the characters around him?

    b. What is the action of the scene?

c. Where is the character (is it a public or private place; is it familiar or foreign)?

d. When does the scene take place (what happened right before, or what is about to happen)?

2. Looking at your list of given circumstances, write down how you think each one will affect your character's movement and speech. A fact is useless if it does not affect the body or voice of a character.

Traps

There are social and mechanical traps for actors who make the switch from working externally to internally. The social traps come from how we are brought up. We are taught from a very young age to categorize people very quickly. For example, we put the people we meet into compartments based on their size, their color, their religion, their economic background, or any number of other factors. Much of the external evidence is used either for or against the people we encounter in order to help us determine how to "deal" with them. The same applies to the characters we play. Dracula is evil, Eliza Doolittle is poor, Tybalt is hot-tempered, and our Modern Millie is spunky. The problem is, actors cannot play "spunky" because spunky means ten different things to ten different people. The other issue is evil, poor, and hot-tempered are not realities; they are judgments, and they are creation killers.

The mechanical traps come when a character's speech pattern or physicality is passed down from a previous performance. Consider the falsetto cackle of Amadeus in Peter Schaffer's play of the same name, or the breathy lisp of Audrey from Little Shop of Horrors. Granted, Salieri speaks of Mozart's laugh in one of his speeches, but I have easy money riding on hundreds of actor's copying Tom Hulce instead of coming up with a laugh of their own design. Actors are interpretive artists, and taking on the physical or vocal characteristics of a character just because a previous (and often inspired) actor has done it isn't acting. It's mimicry, and it doesn't have a place within a live performance.[3] On any given night, An audience should be able to see ten different productions of Hamlet, performed ten different ways.

While it is important for actors to know how other characters in a play feel about the role the actor is playing, it is a deathtrap to base an entire performance on a handful of judgments. The result is typically a two-dimensional performance. I would like to go back to Ellen Greene's performance of Audrey in *Little Shop of Horrors* as an example. It is an iconic piece of musical theatre, and people flock to it. Why? Because she talks funny? Because she wears skimpy skirts? We all know that isn't the reason, or do we? Judging by the countless recreations of her character that have fallen hopelessly flat (from community theatre to Broadway and back again), I would say the majority of young actresses base their characterizations on the idea that all it takes to pull off a fluffy, vacuous, musical theatre character like Audrey is some creative mimicry. Audrey is ditzy, or timid, or sexy. She has a low self esteem, or she makes bad choices. These are character choices grounded in judgments. None of which build a solid character.

It is important then, when taking on a role, to avoid asking what our character is like, but rather why our character is perceived to be that way. Let us work our way through Audrey to see if we can somehow find the third dimension. The first step is to look at the facts. She has a boyfriend who has a well-respected, high paying job. This same boyfriend beats her with his fists and his words. She is poor and lives

22

on skid row. She dreams of getting away from skid row to "Somewhere that's green." She lives in the "early part of a decade, not too long before our own."[4] Perhaps you'll grant me the 1950's. She works at a flower shop who hasn't seen a customer in recent history. These are the realities of Audrey. With these realities we can use Constantin Stanislavski's "Magic If"[5] to see where Ellen Greene built her character.

The "If", for those not familiar, is an integral part of Stanislavski's method of acting. He posited that an actor, through belief in the realities of his character, could ask himself, "What would I *do* if I were stuck in these realities?"[5] It's the doing of actions that make a character in a play worth watching. The realities (always gleaned from the text) determine the intensity, the timing, and the method of each action a character makes. This is where the difference lies in an actor doing what he thinks he is *supposed* to do vs. a character doing what he *has* to do. If I were playing Audrey, I would look for any way out of skid row I could find. I don't have much education, so a high-paying job is out. That leaves finding someone outside of the slums, but how? The answer is simple for someone built like me, but there is a downside to it. The type of guy who is only looking for a curvy body isn't going to treat me with respect, and he may have issues of his own. Once I find this someone, I need to woo him. In *Little Shop*, I have already found this boyfriend; however, each time I see him I am not sure if he will beat me or kiss me. I would do everything in my power to get him to do the latter, and here we see the character emerge. I would dress how he wanted: high heels, short skirts, and a blouse that "flaunts what I got." I would speak in a small voice, so as not to upset him: here is Ellen's choice to use a squeaky, breathy voice (watch her performance for when this voice goes away). I would be ruled by fear: Ellen will jump at every loud noise and sudden movement, not because it's funny, but because she never knows where the next blow is coming from. Bit by bit, we come from the inside to the creation of the character in *Little Shop* we've all come to admire. Actor and character have merged. Behavior replaces posture, motivation replaces duty, and empathy replaces judgment.

THE ACTOR'S HOMEWORK

1. Examine a character you are currently researching, describe how he is typically judged by an audience.

2. Using the list of judgments, justify each one with a fact (or facts) from the text. If you cannot find a suitable fact, perhaps the judgment is unfounded or founded on the performance of another actor (and not the character himself).

3. Now that you have a large base of facts for your character, use that base to ask the next question: If this is true, what else is true? This next step is tricky because you cannot step outside the world of the play, but the answers you get may not be found directly in the text. Use the given circumstance "when" as an example. The text says the action of the scene takes place in 1604. If that is true, then there is a new King in England. Information can only travel as fast as a horse or a ship. Also, whether you are Catholic or Protestant has an increased influence on your well-being.

Empathy Beyond the Stage

For a Christian, the concept and practice of empathy should come easily. Christians tend to miss out on having empathy for their characters from a lack of acting role models. However, most performers (and I would say most people) aren't aware that the greatest actor the world has ever seen is the main character in the Bible. In no way am I claiming Jesus pretended to be human; I will argue that Jesus *became* human. Christ gives us an example of empathy in its purest form. In order to relate to us God's message of redemption by grace through faith, He stepped out of Godhood and into our human shoes. In Philippians 2, we see this process in brief:

> "...who, although He (Jesus) existed in the form of God, did not regard equality with God a thing to be grasped, but emptied Himself, taking the form of a bondservant, and being made in the likeness of men. Being found in appearance as a man, He humbled Himself by becoming obedient to the point of death, even death on a cross."(NASB)[6]

When Jesus took on the role of a human being He approached it with empathy rather than judgment. In John 12, He says:

> "If anyone hears My (Jesus') sayings and does not keep them, I do not judge him; for I did not come to **judge** the world, but to save the world. He who rejects Me and does not receive My sayings, has one who judges him; the word I spoke is what will judge him at the last day. For I did not speak on My own initiative, but the Father Himself who sent Me has given Me a commandment as to what to say and what to speak." (Emphasis added, NASB)[7]

I feel the need to point out here that this role was so defined that it even came with lines (we will explore this concept in the Inspiration chapter).

Why was it important that God become a human? According to Romans 6:23, man's relationship with God has been broken through sin. "For the wages of sin is death..." (NASB).[8] Sin is the replacement of God as our source of life, and death is often seen as separation from God's presence. Practically speaking, God then represents both the injured party and the standard by which we are judged. Following the same logic I presented earlier, empathy cannot contain judgment. Therefore, because, "God so loved the world that He gave His only begotten Son...,"[9] that same Son is able to intercede for us. He not only knows what we're going through, He's gone through it Himself. How else would He be able to say a phrase like, "Father, forgive them; for they do not know what they are doing,"[10] during His execution?

Empathy for a character in a play allows a genuine performance, but its real value is to bring us, as humans, to the same place as Jesus on the cross. I hope to point out here that Christ's example is useful in our lives and our art. We don't have to think of the two spheres as separate any more. Just like the actor who has to play a villain must truly understand where that broken individual is coming from, we must learn to love our enemies by stepping into their shoes. This is also the crux of effective evangelism. We have to not only *know* that someone is hurting, but *why* they are hurting as well. We must learn our fellow human's given circumstances to move beyond pity to ministry. The same questions we would ask to flesh out a character will bring understanding to what is going on in the lives of the people we meet each day. We can relate what Jesus has done for us, and how He has been a part of our lives, but without empathy, we are merely giving good advice instead of good news.

DEVOTIONAL:

1. Read John 4 and examine how Jesus used empathy.

    a. How much did Jesus know about the woman's given circumstances?

    b. How much does Jesus know about your own given circumstances?

2. Is there anyone in your life right now living under your judgment?

    a. Ask God to give you wisdom to understand that person's given circumstances, so you can move toward forgiveness and compassion.

    b. Look for an opportunity to act upon the forgiveness.

Objectives and Empathy: Super Objectives

Understanding where a character is and what has happened to him is only the first part in building a character. Characters, like all people, want something. Sometimes that want is weak, and sometimes it's strong. When preparing for a role, an actor should consider three types of wants for his character. These wants are often called objectives, and they determine how the character moves through the play.

The three objectives are different in size, and they will affect the preparation process differently. The largest and most abstract objective is what Stanislavski called, "the super objective."[5] The next step

27

down is called, "the scene objective," and the most immediate objective is called, "the tactical objective." Think about the objectives as concentric circles that drive each moment of the play.

The Three Objectives

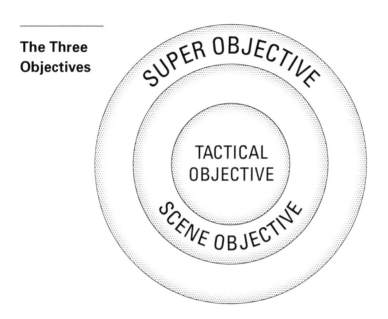

The super objective is the character's ultimate goal within the world of the play. The character may or may not end up at this point, but it's what each scene he is in builds toward. The further away the character gets from the super objective, the harder he will fight to get closer to the objective the next time he gets on stage. Since the super objective is the largest of the objectives, and needs to sustain the character for the entire length of the play, it is also the most conceptual.

Some people have a tough time with concepts, so another way of thinking of super objectives is to think of basic human desires. Think back to a time before humans needed anything. In the Garden of Eden, mankind was in a state of completion. At the fall of man, though, the sustaining force Adam and Eve had in the garden was severed, and man felt need for the first time.[11] What were those needs? To find the answer, look at what Jesus accomplished on the cross. He filled the need for reconciliation, He conquered death, He provided justification/sanctification, He freed us from the slavery of sin, and He gave humanity something to believe in. In a good play, the protagonist's super objective will fall into one of these categories. In a great play, the playwright will make the super objective nearly impossible to achieve. The trick for the performer is to pick the most challenging super objective possible because the harder the character has to fight, the crazier the choices the character is willing to make to achieve his objective. Actors should study the entire play to see which of the five categories (reconciliation, death, justification/sanctification, freedom/control, and faith[12]) most suit his character.

When finding the super objective of the character, always begin with the facts. The character's history, location, and moment before/after tell a lot about what he may want out of the play. Those three facts will also tell how the actor will perform the action of the character. For example, the script may have a character sweeping the floor. If it's a princess who has been kicked out of her kingdom, in a dungeon, in the middle of the winter, right after she's been told that she'll never see her family again, she will sweep differently than the eight year-old boy, who has swept floors all his life in the local wizard's study, who just sneaked a magical broom out of the cupboard. Those two characters will also want vastly different things. The princess may want reconciliation with her family, to save the lives of her subjects, to prove to her kingdom she is the rightful heir, or to find a way to survive in her new circumstances with her heart intact. The young boy, however, might want the wizard to adopt him, to fend off the crazed magical broom, to master the magic behind the broom, or to believe he was destined for something greater than sweeping floors for the rest of his days. All five of those possibilities land within the parameters of the five great needs, so they should be strong enough to push both characters through until the end of the play. Take a look at the needs and see how they play out with a character like Hamlet.

Characters in plays are often looking to mend a relationship, whether it be with themselves or with another character in the world of the play. When forming a usable super objective, it is best to also determine what the accomplishment of that objective looks like. Is reconciliation a hug? Is it an apology? Is it the prevention of a divorce? What does it look like if the other character is dead? Hamlet finds himself in this predicament. How does he reconcile his relationship with his dead father? What does that forgiveness look like? The Father/Son relationship is a powerful one. A strong case could be made for Hamlet's desire to reconcile with his mother, as well. These drives have to be powerful enough to get both our characters and our audiences through four hours of Shakespeare.

Death is a major motivating factor, and it can be used in both of its directions. A character can be avoiding death, whether it's his own death or the death of someone around him; or a character can want to bring death to himself or someone else. One of the ways to twist this need is to add a factor. For example: because dying happens to all living things, the desire to meet death with peace works as a strong objective. If Hamlet is staged as a revenge play, Hamlet's objective can be to bring death to Claudius and anyone else who wronged Hamlet Sr.. On the other hand, Hamlet can see the current regime as a sort of death for his people, so his objective can be to preserve the life of his kingdom. Pursuing death could also be a strong choice. In fact, one of Hamlet's greatest speeches is about the question of whether he should live or die.

When students study Hamlet in class, the question arises: Why does he hesitate? It could be that killing Claudius doesn't seem like the best way to reconcile with his father, or that he wants a particular kind of death for Claudius (both are backed up in the text). However, it could be that Hamlet is looking for justification for his actions. If he goes through with regicide/patricide/treason he needs to know (and he needs his kingdom to know) that there were good reasons for it. The more respect a character has for the opposing character, the more seriously he will undertake the challenge of obtaining justification. It's different explaining to your dog why you were late than it is explaining to a deity.

The desire for control is a motivator that can provide a great many choices for the actor. He can attempt to control people, situations, or even the natural world. It also makes an interesting super objective because control of any one of those things is nearly unattainable. The more difficult the objective, the more creative (and desperate) a character becomes as he strives towards it.

Hamlet's life is out of control from the moment the play opens. Strange weather patterns, ghosts walking about, and a nation on the brink of war with its neighbor set the stage for an even greater amount of chaos. One can argue that Hamlet, after being a pawn in Claudius' and Polonius' political maneuvering, chooses his death in the final scene of the play as his ultimate attempt to meet both life and death on his own terms.

Lastly, a character can wrestle for the right to believe that there is more to life than this "...mortal coil."[13] The need to believe in something is arguably the toughest super objective to cram into a character's brain, but it is one of the most powerful because it lies at the foundation of all the other needs. Hamlet needs to believe he will be reconciled with his family, he needs to believe that death can be conquered, he needs control, and he needs to believe that if he does what he sets out to do, he will be justified. Belief is also core to the Christian worldview. There are many passages in the Bible citing faith and belief as the ingredients for salvation. Even people outside of Christianity justify their actions according to their belief systems. Therefore, Hamlet can go through the internal struggle of the big speeches and come out the other side because he believes the world should operate differently than its current state. He believes it so much, he's willing to pay for it with his life.

The point of finding a specific super objective is less about getting it right and more about giving the actor and director what they both want most: choices. Find a couple of options from each of the four needs, get them on their feet, and see which one resonates with you and the rest of the creative team. The process should be fun. That's why we call them plays.

THE ACTOR'S HOMEWORK

1. Find your character's objective by determining at least four possibilities:

    a. What does he want to reconcile?

    b. Who's death does he want to avoid (or bring about)?

    c. Who/what does he need justification/sanctification from?

    d. How does his faith need to be renewed or changed?

Objectives and Empathy: Scene Objectives

The scenic objective operates like a super objective, but its scope is smaller. Scenic objectives last for an entire French scene (delineated by the entrance or exit of another character), and they must have opposition. Phrase a scenic objective using the following template:

"I want to convince _____ to/that _____."

There are two main reasons to phrase an objective this way. Using the word "convince" forces the objective deeper than a physical objective. For instance, if Anthony wants Cleopatra to leave him alone, he can simply walk out of the room. However, if Anthony wants to convince Cleopatra that she needs to leave the room, then tactical dialogue is required. The second reason to use "convince" is that it implies a change of heart, which is what actors should be looking for in a character arc. Each time a character changes, he gets closer or further away from his super objective. Each change will then affect how the character walks and talks in the subsequent scene. Following these changes through to the climax for the character allows the actor to easily justify whatever actions the character makes to grab for his super objective. This is why villains can monologue and heroes can give their lives. They are either convinced that nothing stands in their way, or that nothing else has worked so far.

Objectives and Empathy: Obstacles

The primary function for a scenic objective is to give a character drive and propel them toward his super objective. Its secondary function is almost equally important. An objective must also create conflict, and to do that it must be in polar opposition to the scene partner's objective. If one character's objective is to convince his mother that admitting her guilt will save her soul, the character's mother's objective must be to convince her son that admitting her guilt will not save her soul. Direct opposition is imperative. If the mother chooses to convince her son that he's a liar, or that she isn't guilty, then the objectives aren't in opposition, and the acting choices are fuzzy. Therefore, actors should work together to find their objectives. An actor can choose for his character to have a hidden agenda, but keeping the objective to himself robs his partner of the tools she needs for a compelling scene. For example, Iago wants to destroy Othello in almost every scene they share. The actor playing Iago can have any number of secrets from his scene partner as to why he's doing the things he's doing, but they can work together to find the conflict in the scene. The actor playing Iago can tell the actor playing Othello that in this particular scene Iago wants to convince Othello that Cassio can't be trusted. Othello can then convince Iago that Cassio can be trusted, and the scene stays clean. In fact, if Iago plays this objective, and leaves all the secrets out of the scene, it will make the final betrayal that much more effective because Iago won't be indicating anything but absolute friendship to his scene partner.

The scene partner's objective is blocking the actor's way to the character's goal. Blockages are called obstacles, and there are two types: internal and external. The most obvious external obstacle is the scene partner's objective. If the only obstacle in place was the opposing objective, and the two characters had equal power, the scene wouldn't go anywhere. For example, consider the famous balcony scene from Romeo and Juliet[14]. If Romeo wants to convince Juliet that one kiss won't hurt, then Juliet would have to convince Romeo that one kiss would do a great deal of damage. The objectives are polar opposites, and in this scene, they carry equal weight. Graphically, it would look something like this:

Diagram I of a Scenic Objective

Scene partner as primary obstacle

Convince Juliet that one kiss won't hurt

Convince Romeo that one kiss can do a lot of damage

However, a scene needs more pull to be interesting, and that is why actors have to search for compelling obstacles. One of the first places an actor should look is the environment. The character may have a condition which prevents him from moving and talking freely. For example, Lavinia, in Shakespeare's *Titus Andronicus*, needs to convince her father to take revenge on Demetrius and Chiron, but her tongue and hands have been removed.[15] Romeo is trying to convince Juliet that one kiss won't hurt, but there are several environmental challenges in his way. The nurse is calling from the next room; Juliet is on (at least) the second floor of the house, and Romeo is on the ground; it's improper for a man to visit a woman alone; it's night time, and Juliet's family will kill him if they find him.

Diagram II of a Scenic Objective

External obstacles

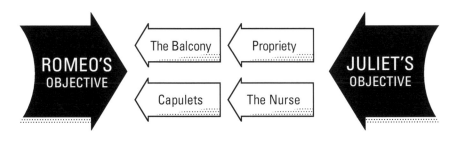

Like external obstacles, internal obstacles pull the character away from his objective. Unlike external obstacles, though, these blockages come from inside the character. In other words, they are the character's doubts and fears. In class we call an internal obstacle "The But..." "The But" fights against the character's objective, but unlike an opposing objective, it isn't bound to be completely opposite. For example, Juliet wants to convince Romeo that a kiss can do great harm, BUT he is incredibly attractive. Part of the fun of character building is finding the internal obstacle (or obstacles) in the scene that is just right. Finding someone attractive is a decent obstacle, but there is probably another, far more active and interesting reason for Juliet to keep Romeo around (even though she knows better). Our diagram changes now to look something like this:

Diagram III of a Scenic Objective
Juliet's internal obstacles balance Romeo's external obstacles

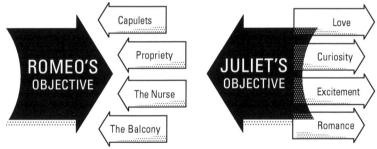

Now the forces are more balanced. We know from reading the script that Romeo eventually leaves, implying Juliet wins this scene. Romeo loses because he has far more obstacles both internal and external fighting against him (see the figure below). Though Romeo doesn't manage to convince Juliet that a kiss won't hurt, he does get a small kiss, an indicator of how close he comes to achieving his goal. In spite of his tremendous need, however, he retreats. Despite his loss, Romeo's super objective is strong enough to keep him coming back.

Diagram IV of a Scenic Objective
Romeo's greater obstacles defeat him

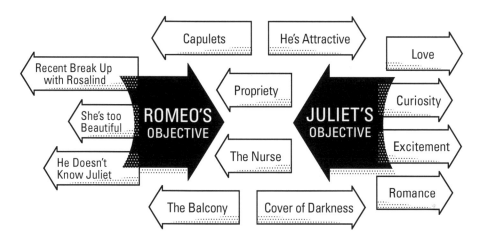

THE ACTOR'S HOMEWORK

1. What are your character's objectives for each scene?

2. How does your objective inform your character's actions?

3. Is your objective something your scene partner can directly fight against?

4. How does utilizing the phrase "to convince" help determine objectives?

5. What are your character's internal and external obstacles?
    Fill in the blanks:

I want to convince my scene partner to/that _____,

but _____.

Objectives and Empathy: Tactics

There is one more reason to use the word convince when phrasing an objective. It implies a need for a scene partner. So often, actors feel like they are working in a vacuum, and it leads to a self-centered approach to performance. One way around selfish acting is to aim all of your objectives squarely at your scene partner. If you need to convince the character you are acting with that she needs to leave her boyfriend and run away with you, you won't know if you are making any progress unless you are listening to her with your whole body. Whatever responses she is giving you will fuel the next tactic you use on her. This is what I meant earlier when I mentioned tactical dialogue.

If every character has opposing objectives, the actors (through the characters) must adapt to the moves made by their scene partners. These movements and adaptations are called tactics. Just like objectives, tactics are based on the given circumstances of the character. If the character is a 5' tall drill sergeant on the first day of boot camp, and he needs to convince his new recruits that he is not their caretaker, he will employ active verbs like, intimidate, humiliate, or obliterate to affect his scene partners. He will attack his scene partners, working on their weaknesses, or responding to their reactions. Notice I did not say he should yell at them. Yelling may happen, but deciding to yell simply because it sounds good leads to self-indulgent acting.

When an actor plans to yell at another actor, he will take a larger breath, activate his resonators, and make his face angry. All of those actions take the actor into himself and away from the scene. Therefore, just like objectives, an actor should focus his tactics on his scene partner and use his voice, however he needs to, in order to affect his partner's performance. Think about the words intimidate, humiliate, and obliterate used in the drill sergeant scenario. These are all words that can be done to someone else, and each one comes with a response the drill sergeant is hoping to illicit from his scene partners.

Look at another example of tactical dialogue: Imagine a freshman girl, away from home for the first time. She has never wanted for anything until this moment. Her luggage has been lost, her roommate has been switched with a girl who blares death metal non-stop, she hasn't slept in two days, her boyfriend just broke up with her an hour ago, and she just got called on in class and had no clue what the professor was talking about. A self-centered actor would get ready for her crying scene. An other-centered actor would think tactically. *Should I look for pity from the professor or the class? Should I bluff the professor? Should I attack the professor?* Some of these tactics may involve shedding a tear, some lean toward holding it together. The point, though, is that the actor isn't thinking, "Here comes my big crying scene. Oh, I hope I get some tears out. When is she going to be done talking, so I can cry?" On the contrary, the actor is completely involved in moving the scene forward. In fact, if the director wants tears in the scene, it's not really the freshman girl's responsibility. The professor needs to step up her tactical game and play something like "to crush," or "to decimate."

If coming up with active verbs (or using them) is difficult, flip them around. Instead of using a verb, go for a physical or verbal response from your scene partner. This is the third and most specific of all of the objectives, or the tactical objective. Instead of using "to scare," try to get your scene partner to back up a few steps. Instead of using "to seduce," get your scene partner to come forward or lean in. Eliciting anything, from a widening of the eyes, to a hug, to a full out scream, can be a tactical objective. The more specific the tactical objective, the clearer the acting is to the audience. The benefit of working towards a response from your scene partner is you have the opportunity to surprise yourself with how much effort it takes to get them to move. Those are the moments actors and audiences are in true communion because both of them are experiencing the performance at the exact same time. The performance can stay both fresh and reliable, even over a longer run. Using active verbs or tactical objectives to get your scene objective is a terrific way of shifting the spotlight off your own performance and on to the performance of your supporting cast.

The benefit of building a character using empathy, is that the given circumstances feed directly into determining all three of the character's different objective types. This process requires time and critical thinking because most of the answers you are looking for won't be directly stated on the page. If you are disciplined about this type of work, though, line memorization problems will be minimal due to the extraordinary amount of time spent in the text. Secondly, if your given circumstances are deep and applicable, and if you fully invest belief in your super/scenic/tactical objectives, the lines the playwright gave you should come naturally. Do this work before the first rehearsal, and your performance will have one fewer roadblock in its way.

THE ACTOR'S HOMEWORK

1. What are the tactics your character uses on your scene partner? Use active verbs.

2. What are the tactics your scene partner uses on you?

3. How do you expect your scene partner's character to react to your tactics? Make your tactical objective a specific physical or vocal reaction.

CHAPTER 3

Fear

"Fear is the path to the dark side. Fear leads to anger,
anger leads to hate, hate leads to suffering." [1]

– Yoda

The Problem of Fear

What Master Yoda left out was, "Fear also leads to a stunted and painful performance." Where God's love enables and empowers, fear shuts down or undercuts performances. Granted, performers have plenty of reasons to be afraid. They constantly face rejection, unemployment, and they step into situations where their safety can be on the line. People will not willingly put themselves in the path of danger, so when an actor enters a fearful situation, her body (naturally) wants to be left behind. This causes a problem because the actor's body is the gateway for the audience into the world of the play. When the actor's body is in a scene but her brain is in the audience, or in the next scene, or in the monologue she just botched, the gateway closes, and the audience is left out of the experience.

But where does fear get its start? Chemically, fear starts in the portions of the brain called the amygdala and the hippocampus. These two parts of the brain are responsible for emotional memory formation and storage. The hippocampus forms the memory of the experience, and the amygdala remembers the context.[2] In short, emotional memory is what keeps people out of harm's way. For example, a child puts his hand on a hot stove; not only does he get a painful burn, but the two hard-to-pronounce areas of the brain store the experience in the child's memory (hippocampus) and give her a healthy respect for kitchens and stoves (amygdala). The same is true for performers. As much as they love to be loved, they have an unequaled fear of rejection. At some point in each performer's life, a joke has fallen flat, or a note has come out sour, or a line has been completely forgotten. The audience laughed at the wrong moment, or maybe they didn't laugh at all. The experience was seared into the memory, and the context was remembered as well: "I was in front, and there were people watching." That is all it takes for the performer's body to instinctively go into "fear mode."

To bring fear into an audition or performance can only end in frustration. Perhaps you can relate. You're up next, and the first thing to go is your breath. You can't seem to get enough air, so you begin to push. Your heart picks up speed to compensate for the low oxygen levels, and most of the blood is diverted to the muscles (not the brain). This chain of events causes your limbs to shake, your chest to cramp, and your temperature to fluctuate. Finally, your stomach chimes in. It can't do its job under these conditions, and it decides to empty itself. At this point, you can only hope you had a light lunch. And here is your cue...

THE ACTOR'S HOMEWORK

1. Think back to your last audition or performance when you experienced fear.

2. What was your body's response?

3. What was your mind's response?

4. What are your performance related fears?

5. Outside of a theatrical experience, how do you respond to fear? What are the similarities to how you respond in performance?

The Spiritual Response

The previous list of symptoms are activated by what experts call the "fight or flight" response. In practice, an anxious actor will either want to punch her scene partners in the neck or run screaming from the theatre. Perhaps you've witnessed a performer throw a fit about staging or how her dressing room doesn't have the correct number of hangers. Fear tells actors they won't succeed with the hand they're dealt, so they act out. They lie on their resume or steal material. Science tell us these behaviors are perfectly normal. This bit of insight may help us out. Knowing these actors are operating from a place of fear will allow Christian performers to have a little empathy for them instead of writing them off as "divas" or "hacks."

That said, understanding the neuroses of others is only one aspect of dealing with fear in a professional setting. A solution must be found to our anxieties, so we can then react instead from a place of security. I see a two part solution: half spiritual and half physical, but the spiritual side must be dealt with first. The solution to the spiritual aspect can be found in the book of 1st John. There is encouragement in chapter 4 where it says, "He who is in you is greater than he who is in the world (vs. 4)."[3] We are also told that, "Perfect love casts out fear (vs. 18)."[3] John then lets us know how to experience this perfect love in verse 16. He says to, "…rely on the love God has for us."[3] Simply put, love is the cure for fear, and reliance on love is how to put the cure to work. Note that John does not weigh all loves equally. He is specific about the importance of the perfect love of *God*. It may seem too abstract or cliché to say, "I need to rely on God's love more." However, the concept becomes more concrete if you think of it not as a new condition, but as a *shift* of reliance from one thing to another. Too many performers rely upon the love of their craft, of their fans, or of their natural abilities. All of these have a tendency to dissipate, delude, or disappoint. To drive fear completely from your life can only be done through the "perfect love" offered by God through a relationship with His Son.

False Security

Why then are Christian actors ruled by fear? We're human. We've all had our connection with God severed at one point. When afraid, we tend to cling to what we can see or touch, much like a drowning sailor embraces a floating plank. Imagine anything but perfect love as the sailor's ship. It feels sturdy. It protects him. It takes him places and offers a sense of home. When it is shattered by a powerful storm, the sailor will hold on to the wreckage of his past security and drift at the mercy of the current, or worse, at the whim of the storm. All of the different sources of love I just mentioned (the work, the applause, and the body) offer some level of comfort and confidence, but like the ship, none of them is invincible.

Let us first consider reliance on the work. Actors, at best, are temp workers, and even more are regularly unemployed. A job can last anywhere from months to just a single day. When actors do book a job, it can sometimes be tedious or even demeaning. And what happens when the work isn't there at all? It is easy to compare yourself to working friends and to grow disenchanted with your own circumstances. On the other side, booking consistent work may inflate the ego, making you harder to work with, causing longer gaps between jobs, beginning the cycle of unemployment all over again. Work has too many variables to put any serious faith into it.

Even shakier is reliance on the love applause offers us. People imagine life in the entertainment industry as a glamorous roller coaster of fun, lit by the flashbulbs of the paparazzi. They imagine hoards of screaming fans who follow their every move. I have a few problems with this supposition. First, the attention some celebrities get is not the type of attention most people want. The supermarket checkout line is choked with headlines of divorce, addiction, and scandal. The last thing I need are blurry pictures of my thighs with a red circle around them telling the world I'm too fat or too skinny. Second, the reality is that a vast majority of working actors have little to no name and face recognition. After opening night, the crowds of friends and supporters trickle away, and the stage door can become a lonely place. Lastly, to balance out the applause, God has created a breed of humans whose sole purpose is to feed on the blood of actors. The critic will fatten up an actor with a modicum of praise and, with hardly any provocation at all, will tear an actor's psyche to shreds. Tim Keller pointed out in a sermon named after Kierkegaard's, *A Sickness Unto Death*,[4] that outward applause and inner applause have a nasty habit of disappearing. The newspaper clippings fade, the Google searches turn up fewer results, and the next performance falls flat.

Surely, the actor's body, the one arena over which she has some control can be relied upon. I thought so until I was forced to take a hiatus from acting in 2005. I had to stop everything I was doing due to an illness which lasted for the better part of a year. I wasn't a person who took poor care of his body. I was in shape; I was young, but there I was, hunched over a toilet for hours each day, watching everything on which I based my significance flush away. My instrument, my body, was essentially taken away from me and put on a shelf.

If I had clung to the wreckage of my fans, or my body, or my craft, I would have floated away or sunk. Throughout the downtime I was very hard on myself, and unhappiness plagued me. When I heard other people talk about their successes as performers, I would either sneer at them and their level of mediocrity, or at myself for letting my career go to seed. What happens if no one remembers you? What happens if no one likes you anymore? What if you cannot physically continue performing? There has to be something better than human-generated applause because circumstances change. Thankfully, I eventually traded a floating plank for a rock on which to build my home that will never sink, never fade, and never leave me adrift. I found a source of eternal, continual applause.

True Security

Fear is the opposite of faith. Fear says, "Look out! Something inescapably bad is on its way, and it is gunning for me." Faith says, "Even though things look bad, I will not be destroyed. God is with me, and He is giving me the chance to wholly rely on Him. I need to be where I am right now for the perfection of my soul." The Bible is clear that it isn't the size or power of one's faith that matters, it is the size and power of the faith's focus. An actor can have tremendous confidence in her popularity, her body, or her craft, but those things are all limited. They have no capacity to look out for her or influence anything outside their immediate sphere. Conversely, an actor can have a mustard seed's worth of faith in the God of the Bible, and mountains will move.[5]

DEVOTIONAL

1. What is your first response to fear? Who/where do you go first for comfort?

2. What Biblical promises do you know that address fear? Read them in context and see if there are even more insights for dealing with fear.

3. How does fear keep you from taking chances on stage?

4. How does fear keep you from sharing your faith?

The Physical Response to Fear

Once the spiritual side of fear has been dealt with, the physical aspect can be addressed. There are two sides to all of us: the flesh and the soul. These two parts do not communicate well with each other because the flesh is ruled by self preservation, and it has no way of knowing it won't be eaten when it enters the audition room. All of the physical sensations you feel when stage-fright kicks in have been honed over eons by the human instinct to dodge saber-toothed cats. This is handy for keeping you alive and ripping car doors off their hinges, but it can be disastrous in performance. The problem with instincts is they have the critical thinking skills of a doorpost. The good news is, as easy as it is for your fight or flight response to be fooled into thinking your body is in danger, it is equally easy to fool it back the other way.

The general method for conquering the jitters is to take care of the initial physical reaction. When under attack, the breath seems to be the first thing to go. This comes from the body demanding more oxygen for handling the stressful situation coupled with our tendency to hold our breath. A simple relaxation exercise does wonders for reigning in adrenaline. There are as many different relaxation methods as there are performers, but they all have the common goal of calming these three common elements: the brain, the breath, and the body. Below is a suggested regimen:

- *Focus on the moment* (*the brain*) – This is your chance to reason with your body before you resort to physical trickery. The present moment remembers no lack of preparation, and there is no fear of potential consequences. There is only the now, and the now comes with a task that needs to be done. When you are auditioning, performing, or meeting an agent, gently remind yourself that you are there because God put you there, "For such a time as this."[6] Your shortcomings do not matter because God can use anyone, and there are no consequences God can't handle. Also, the casting director, the agent, and the audience aren't going to jump out of their seats and attack you. I like this image because it always makes me laugh. Laughter is a great stress reliever, and it forces the body to take in a cleansing breath.

- *Take a cleansing breath* (*the breath*) – This is a basic component used in Yoga and Lamaze. The object is to "clean" out the old, stale air and carbon dioxide sitting in your lungs. This breath should really begin with an expulsion of air. To get the lungs truly empty, try bending at the waist as though your body were a bellows, and exhale in short, sharp bursts until your lungs are empty. You can either be sitting or standing. The trick is to make sure you are bending at the waist and not your back. Think of bending from the hips if it helps. It may also help to "hiss" out the breath through your teeth. The next part is a slow inhalation through the nose. The back of the throat should be wide open, and you should be able to feel the cooler air rush deep into your lungs. To get the fullest breath you can, engage your diaphragm (your stomach will stick out). This will cause the diaphragm to act as a vacuum for your lungs. You may also want to come back to an upright position, but it isn't necessary. Exhale with the hissing and repeat.

- ***Tension and release*** *(the body)* – This exercise can be done standing or lying down. It is wise to also incorporate the previous two exercises with this one. Keep your mind from wandering into the future or the past, and keep utilizing the cleansing breath (focusing on the breath is a great way to keep your brain in check). From either position you choose, start flexing your toes. As you flex (tension), keep a nice, slow breath coming in. When you relax (release), exhale slowly and completely. Next, flex your toes and your arches. Then release them. Move your way up and through your body, adding a small body part each time (add the calves, then the thighs, then the glutes, etc.). I find it useful to hold my breath at the pinnacle of the tension when I am flexing a sore or sleepy body part; then I exhale when I feel I have fully tensed that particular muscle group. It is important to note that I do not suggest you tense your neck. Actors carry around enough stress in their neck, we don't have to artificially add more. If at any point you are unable to take in air while flexing a muscle (this happens in the chest most often), you are not flexing correctly. Experiment with your muscles to see how to get your lungs working at the same time.

These three exercises do everything adrenaline does without the tunnel vision and unpleasant after effects (nausea, dizziness, muscle cramping). You are focusing your mind, and circulating oxygen rich blood to every pocket of your body. The whole process can take less than 7 minutes, but it can last as long as you want. Like I said before, there are thousands of variations of relaxation techniques. Make your own version that suits you best, but be sure it takes care of the three B's: the brain, the breath, and the body.

THE ACTOR'S HOMEWORK

1. Each time you do the tension and release exercise, take a mental inventory of your body both before and afterwards.

2. What parts of your body have tension?

3. Which sections of your body were hardest to isolate?

4. Which sections of your body made it difficult to breathe while applying tension?

5. Do you have your own method for preparing the brain, the breath, and the body? What are the pros and cons of each method? How can you merge both methods?

The Arenas of Fear: The Audition

In addition to a general relaxation technique, there are some specific things we can do to calm down based on the brand of fear you are experiencing. In order to deal effectively with a particular fear, it helps to know the specific arena each brand comes from.

Job interviews are the worst. First of all, you are most likely at the interview because you are out of work, or you are dissatisfied with your current job. Then, you are expected to walk into a small room with a couple of people you've never met and convince them how great you are. By far, the most unsettling part of the interview process is the waiting room. Here is where all of the malevolent "if's" fester and spread in your mind, and the unknown becomes a malevolent, palpable, force. Imagine having to interview for work every eight weeks, having to constantly prove your worth to a new set of producers who may or may not care how critically acclaimed your last performance was. Worst of all, in the waiting room are fourteen carbon copies of yourself, and most of them are muttering noiselessly to themselves as if they were all shell-shocked in a rice patty in Vietnam.

The audition room can be a fearful place even for experienced actors. There are several factors contributing to an actor's trepidation upon entering "the room." Let's start with a few of the factors over which a performer has some control and see if the Bible has something to say about them.

I have been a reader for a large number of auditions where the first words out of the performer's mouth were, "I've been sick for the last few days," or my favorite, "My agent didn't get me the sides until last night." It is common for actors to sandbag their performance. Rare is the moment in time where you are at your absolute physical, mental, financial, relational, spiritual peak, all of which have a profound effect on your performance. However, it is important to note that casting directors do not find sandbags endearing.

There is no excuse for ill-preparedness. Colossians 3:23 plainly states for whom the Christian performer is working, and this boss has incredibly high standards. Christians in the arts need to be more prepared than others because they are representing more than just themselves. It is important to remember that God is not helping us so we can have a juicier role in some show, but rather He is giving us the tools necessary to join in the plans He has laid out for us. The less we prepare, the more we show God our unwillingness to be a part of the work He will accomplish in the world.

What happens then if you aren't ready, and it truly is not your fault? In situations like this, I look to the book of Judges, starting in chapter 6, at a man named Gideon. Here was a man who had an appointment, who prepared for his appointment, and before he arrived, God took most of his resources away. Once it was clear to Gideon that he was going to be the one fighting, *but not the one responsible for the outcome*, he was able to trust in God and give God glory for any success that came his way.[7] I see this all the time when traffic, family, or even the weather conspire to prevent me from attending or preparing for an audition. The fact is, we *will* be late. Computers *will* fail. We *will* have circumstances beyond our control. The trick is to be able to take a look at the series of events which conspired to leave us unprepared and see God stripping us of our earthly crutches to leave us completely dependent on Him.[8] The more opportunities you take to trust God, the more trustworthy He seems to become (I say seems because He's not changing, we are).

It might seem odd to mention the response to an audition as something over which an actor has some control. It is true that a performer has little control over the producer's response, but she can, however, have responsibility for her own reactions. How a person will react to her own audition can make a significant difference in whether her day/month/year (dare I say, career) is ruined or launched. Some actors have terrible poker faces. I have seen them melt down in the audition room, or rage at an accompanist, creating an awkward moment for everyone involved. If an actor can nail or bomb a performance with grace, her chances of booking the job increase dramatically. Producers want talent, but what they want even more is talent who can play well with others. An actor who knows that God will place her exactly where He needs her, when He needs her there, is able to throw a smile on the end of any audition. Almost as important as the first few seconds in the room, are the last few (even after the door closes behind you), so if you have a hard time putting your best face on after a shaky audition, make Jeremiah 29:11 a part of your life:. "For I know the plans I have for you,' says the Lord, 'plans for welfare and not for calamity, to give you a future and a hope.'"(NASB)[9]

THE ACTOR'S HOMEWORK

1. When fear affects your body, how is your audition affected?

2. How can you avoid fear in your next audition?

3. How can you deal with fears you are unable to avoid?

4. What can you do to ensure you are fully prepared for an audition (see the end of the chapter titled, "Work Ethic" for some ideas).

The Arenas of Fear: The Rehearsal

In an ideal world, the rehearsal space is a sanctuary where actors, directors, and designers come together in a spirit of encouragement and collaboration. However, we do not live in the garden anymore. It is very difficult to shake an actor's need to be liked. Actors bring this need with them wherever they go, and the rehearsal process is no exception. It can take several days before a cast lets its guard down enough to discover anything worthwhile. In an era when rehearsal periods are shrinking, a show cannot afford to waste precious time. Acting teachers have long recognized this problem, hence the endless litany of trust exercises they employ at the beginning of their classes. These exercises range from leading fellow students around blindfolded, to falling backwards into a partner's hands, to exploring one another's personal space. I subscribe to many of these methods, but I also find they lack a certain practicality. It is often easier to trust a new acquaintance to catch you when you are in a controlled environment where the game is, "Catch me when I fall." It is more difficult to have faith your castmate is going to remember all of her lines, or to stay true to all of her fight choreography, or not assassinate you or your performance when your back is turned. In the beginning stages of rehearsal, when trust is either fragile or non-existent, fear seizes control.

Barring preparedness, which we discussed earlier, there are two halves to the fear equation in rehearsal. You will be fearful of everyone in the room, and everyone in the room will be afraid of you. Both of these factors can be trumped, however, by how you deport yourself while working.

And it starts on day one.

There is a trap for actors regarding the work process, and it begins in acting school. For a young theatre student, her life is crammed with classes, work, family, and rehearsal. There is no such thing as free time. The natural result is all of the "work" for a production has to take place at rehearsal. This establishes a pattern, so when the transition is made from student to theatre professional, actors continue to think that work only happens at rehearsal. Not all actors behave in this manner, but it is difficult to trust those who do. When Jack O'Brien was the artistic director at the Old Globe Theatres, he would tell his actors that he could tell the difference between a professional actor and an amateur because the amateur would come to rehearsals ready to do whatever the director told them. The professional, on the other hand, came to work full of choices, a menu as it were, and the director got to pick his favorite. Where are these choices generated if not outside the rehearsal space in the "off time?"

The amateur and the professional come to the rehearsal process from two different perspectives. According to Mr. O'Brien, the amateur comes to be served, and the professional to be a servant. At first glance, the amateur actor may not seem self-centered. On the contrary, she may think she is being extremely gracious. After all, she came in as tabula rasa, and she is "open" to anything. In reality, she is asking the director to hand her the perfect performance. The up-side for the actor is that she can shift credit or blame for a standing ovation or a stinging review to suit her needs. An amateur attitude can also fracture a cast in the same way it affected Jesus' disciples. Look at the book of Mark, chapter 10. Jesus' ensemble is splitting apart because two of the leads attempted a power play over what the theatre would call, "billing."

> "James and John, the two sons of Zebedee, came up to Jesus, saying, "Teacher, we want You to do for us whatever we ask of You."
> And He said to them, "What do you want Me to do for you?"

> They said to Him, "Grant that we may sit, one on Your right and one on Your left, in Your glory." (NASB)[10]

This private moment is followed by a public one. Note that the public moment is what causes the commotion. The other ten disciples see James and John talking with Jesus, and somehow they hear the exchange. A few verses later it says, "…the ten heard about this…" [10] which hints at them finding out about it after the fact. This is one example proving there is no such thing as a truly private moment within a cast, especially a cast as tight as the disciples. The exchange between Jesus, James, and John embitters the rest of the men and threatens to split them into factions. Coming back to the rehearsal room, if everything in the room is treated as public, then there won't be room for secrets. Secrets are poison to an ensemble[11], as we see played out in the next few verses.

Jesus, however, glosses over the external issues, and with His usual wisdom, treats on the core of the problem. We all want to be great. We all want our name in some kind of light. Jesus acknowledges the desire. He doesn't tell His disciples they are wrong to yearn for greatness. Instead, He tells them how greatness is achieved. First, He calls them all together (as an ensemble) and redefines what it means to have importance in contrast to the world's definition:

> "You know that those who are recognized as rulers of the Gentiles lord it over them; and their great men exercise authority over them."[10]

Using Jack O'Brien's logic, these guys are amateurs. Then, Jesus sets His men apart: "But it is not this way among you…"[10]

In an instant, He takes a group of jealous men and elevates them to something unified and unique. This is an example of a great director at work. Then, Jesus gives the solution to the fear present in the first week of rehearsal.

"...but whoever wishes to become great among you shall be your servant; and whoever wishes to be first among you shall be slave of all." [10]

Be a servant, not a rival. Be a professional, not an amateur. Amateurs are inherently fearful because their position in the hierarchy hasn't yet been established, and they will guard whatever place they hold with tenacity. Professionals, however, are inherently trustworthy because they bring something to the table. You can get a room full of strangers to lose their fear of you if you can convince them you are at rehearsal to be a servant to all, if you bring something to the table instead of expecting something from it. A large part of being a servant is being diligent about the work outside of rehearsal, and coming in with choices for the director and cast to play with. The other part is something people in the acting world call, "taking care of the other guy."

THE ACTOR'S HOMEWORK

1. Evaluate yourself at a rehearsal. Are you waiting to be given your character, or have you brought one of your own.

2. What can you bring to rehearsal that will serve the director, the stage manager, and the rest of the cast?

3. How much time outside of each rehearsal do you take to research and plan?

"Looking out for the other guy"

There is a strain of actor who seems to be immune to fear. They can be found in what some call "theatre without a net." If theatre has an equivalent to extreme sports, it's improvisational comedy. There are no lines, no predetermined characters, and most of the time there is no set. There is nothing but the actors and their willingness to believe in each other. Each night, these actors look failure in the face and come up laughing. How do they do it? Does improv attract fearless actors, or cultivate them?

In Tom Shales and James Andrew Miller's book, *Live From New York: An Uncensored History of Saturday Night Live*, we are given a comprehensive history of one of the most popular television shows in America. The book is a collection of anecdotes and thoughts from the show's producers, stars, writers, and guests. Several of the actors muse on the reasons why some sketches "worked" and others didn't. The overwhelming consensus was that a piece worked when all of the actors were focused on making each other look good.[12] Most of the performers and writers on Saturday Night Live came from a background in improvisation. Though improv appears to be totally free-form, there are several rules the actors follow which give us a clue to how they handle fear. Here are just a few:

- ***Don't Deny:*** This is the rule of never saying "no" to someone's idea in a scene. Rather, the actor's response should be, "Yes, and..." or even better, "If what you did is true, then what else is also true?"

- ***Don't Ask Open Ended Questions:*** The idea behind this is the actor should be giving ideas to her scene partners rather than forcing them to come up with all of their own material. Instead of,

"Where were you?" she can give her partner a boost with, "Did you have fun at the morgue?"

- **Listen:** Listen with your whole body. Listen to the words, the tone, the rhythm, and the body language. You can get everything you need from your partner, and your partner can get everything they need from you. [13]

Each of these points hits on what actors fear most in a rehearsal. They don't want their ideas shot down, but they also don't want the onus of creating a scene to fall solely on their shoulders. Lastly, they want someone to listen to them. It is the keeping of rules like these that make improv actors a joy to work with. The laws point the actors away from themselves and back to the story. They are not concerned about their own spotlight since they spend all of their energy putting a spotlight on their scene partners. You will often hear performers talking about other actors being "giving." They are referring to actors who are dedicated to giving their scene partners everything they need to say their next line or perform their next bit. In brief, a giving actor doesn't need trust, she generates it.

Philippians 2:4 says, "...do not merely look out for your own personal interests, but also for the interests of others." (NASB)[14] Once again, we can back up our acting principle with Scripture. We will return to Philippians often throughout this book because of its incredible relevance to good performance, attitude, and deportment. The concept Paul gives is not new, but it is difficult. However, I cannot think of a better way to "...love your neighbor as yourself." (NASB)[15] than to give your scene partner their next cue along with your ears and your heart. These two biblical tenets are the heart of why training in improvisation is so good at exterminating fear.

I learned this next concept from actor/teacher James Winker as he expounded on a couple of characters from Shakespeare's *Twelfth Night*. He points out that the hardest working actor in the play is the one playing Sir Toby Belch. On the surface, Toby is self-centered, self-indulgent, and just plain cruel (judgments, I know). However, in the play's construction, he plays the straight man to almost all of the play's funniest moments. Nearly all of his lines are oddly worded, obsolete set-ups for other characters' punchlines. Most of the laughs in the show, however, come from the simple, easy to understand, one-liners from Sir Andrew, or the droll reactions of Malvolio. During the curtain call, it is typically Sir Andrew and Malvolio who get screams and applause while Toby is lucky to walk away with a "thank-you-for-coming." Mr. Winker's point, though, was that Toby can only feel like he's done his job if his castmates get the reward. It's beauty and sacrifice at its theatrical finest.

I teach a technique of script scoring in my classes which is designed to change the actor's focus to be on her scene partner. When a script is passed out, the first thing most actors do is highlight their lines. I suggest modifying this practice. Use a highlighter and a pencil to mark the following in the script.:

1. Highlight all of the character's cue lines. Cues are the line of dialogue before and actor speaks

2. Place a box around all of the character's triggers. Triggers are words or actions that force the character to say her next line or perform her next action in the scene.

3. Underline the triggers for the other characters in the scene.

Concentrating more on why your character speaks will keep you listening not for the end of your partner's line, but for the impulses driving the scene. A sample script scoring can be found in the appendix at the end of the book.

Loving your scene partner by ensuring they have all of the reasons they need to speak or move, will take the attention off of yourself and your anxieties won't have any place to grow. Remember, a servant is rarely seen as a rival. Loving your cast with an impeccable work ethic, both inside and outside of the rehearsal room, will allay their fears and take your mind off your own.

THE ACTOR'S HOMEWORK

1. Make a list of all of the circumstances or people that cause you to fear. Can you find a common thread between them?

2. How much do you modify your line delivery based on your scene partner's actions? Think of specific moments where this worked or failed.

3. How much are you able to force your scene partner to modify her line deliveries based on your actions? Think of specific moments where this worked or failed.

The Arenas of Fear: The In-Between Time

What is an actor when she isn't acting? Many actors will tell you the most helpful phrase a performer learns in school is, "Would you like fries with that?" The fact is, there are not many people who have their Equity or SAG cards who are employed as performers. It is hard to stay positive when people ask, "So, what do you do?" and the only answer to give is, "I (blank), but really I'm an actor." Unemployment by itself is scary, and it is made worse by the inordinate amount of hoops actors must jump through just to get an audition. The good news is there are ways to meet this fear, and there is even something to look forward to in the "off times."

The first thing to do when fear comes around is to honestly answer an objective question. Why are you out of work? There are three major reasons actors find themselves unemployed, and each brings its own unique brand of fear with it. Perhaps their show just closed. Maybe they are stuck in the audition process. It is also possible that they cannot even get an audition. All of these scenarios can lead to a nagging depression, feelings of inadequacy or isolation, and a crippling anxiety about the future. Left unchecked, their last show may indeed be their last show.

One of the beautiful things about the theatre is its temporal nature. However, it can also be one of the hardest things to cope with. When a production ends, there is often a mixture of sadness and relief. There are fears that no other show will be like the one that just closed, and sometimes there is the fear the next show will be *just* like it. When coming off a three month job, it helps to remember that temporality is a Biblical concept.

Isaiah 40 shows us the pattern of things coming and going as well as the One responsible for the pattern. From a contextual point of view, this passage is addressed to the Israelites while they are still in captivity. However, it looks forward to a time when, "...her warfare has ended..." The chapter is primarily about the enduring word of God versus the short term realities of man. Taking a look at the entirety of chapter 40 will help us get a handle on experiencing hope in a time of despair.

Whether you feel you have won or lost, a production can give the impression of being through warfare. At the end of the show, remember what Isaiah tells us in chapter 40, verse 6b:

> "All flesh is grass, and all its loveliness is like the flower of the field.
> The grass withers, the flower fades,
> When the breath of the LORD blows upon it;
> Surely the people are grass.
> The grass withers, the flower fades,
> But the word of our God stands forever." (NASB)[16]

Things pass. Good, bad, heartbreaking, breathtaking: all of it passes. When things are bad, remember there is hope. It helps to have a light at the end of the tunnel when under the thumb of a tyrannical director or performing outdoors with swarms of mosquitoes. What is harder to swallow is when the good things wither away. The passage talks about the flesh's "loveliness," and compares it to a, "flower of the field." These are good things. Where is the hope when we are told that all of the good things we do will blow away with the breath of God? Read on to the next stanza, starting in verse 9:

> "Get yourself up on a high mountain,
> O Zion, bearer of good news,
> Lift up your voice mightily,
> O Jerusalem, bearer of good news;
> Lift it up, do not fear.

Say to the cities of Judah,
"Here is your God!"
Behold, the Lord GOD will come with might,
With His arm ruling for Him.
Behold, His reward is with Him
And His recompense before Him.
Like a shepherd He will tend His flock,
In His arm He will gather the lambs
And carry them in His bosom;
He will gently lead the nursing ewes.[16]

Isaiah tells us about good news shouted from the mountain. A shepherd is coming who will "...tend His flock...gather the lambs and carry them in His bosom..."[16] A shepherd's job is to make sure his herd can eat and sleep in peace. He cannot let his sheep graze too long in one area, or the grass there will be completely destroyed. Rather, the good shepherd will keep his flock on the move. It is important to note that this only brings comfort if you buy into the idea of the shepherd. Rogue sheep can go where they please and eat to their heart's content, but they're also easy prey for wolves and their own stupidity. Untended sheep have been known to get their coats caught in bushes and starve, or they've drown because they try to drink running water. You may ask, "If God loves us, then why isn't the next job more certain? Why do the good shows have to end? Why do the bad shows have to come along at all?"

"Who has measured the waters in the hollow of His hand,
And marked off the heavens by the span,
And calculated the dust of the earth by the measure,
And weighed the mountains in a balance
And the hills in a pair of scales?
Who has directed the Spirit of the LORD,
Or as His counselor has informed Him?

With whom did He consult and who gave Him understanding?
And who taught Him in the path of justice
and taught Him knowledge
And informed Him of the way of understanding?
Behold, the nations are like a drop from a bucket,
And are regarded as a speck of dust on the scales;
Behold, He lifts up the islands like fine dust.
Even Lebanon is not enough to burn,
Nor its beasts enough for a burnt offering.
All the nations are as nothing before Him,
They are regarded by Him as less than nothing and meaningless.[16]

Isaiah spends the next five verses, starting in verse 12, telling us the God we think of as bending to our whims and smoothing out our lives is too small. The God who made the universe and measured out the sands of the world is also in charge of your career. His thoughts are going to be bigger than yours; his plans are going to stretch farther. We actors tend to see the world in six to eight week segments. God sees an eternal timeline, so there will be things along the way that won't make sense. Therefore, when good things come to an end, or bad things linger, we feel that somehow God got it wrong. That is the core problem with believing in a sovereign God. You cannot have it half-way. There are people who think they can exercise some control of their gods, but Isaiah makes it clear in verses 16 and 17 that our God cannot be bought. He goes on in verses 18 through 20 to illuminate just how crafting our own compliant god has to be done with care just to keep it from rotting to pieces or falling on its face.

"To whom then will you liken God?
Or what likeness will you compare with Him?
As for the idol, a craftsman casts it,
A goldsmith plates it with gold,

And a silversmith fashions chains of silver.
He who is too impoverished for such an offering
Selects a tree that does not rot;
He seeks out for himself a skillful craftsman
To prepare an idol that will not totter." [16]

Lastly, Isaiah tells us how to endure the times when it seems the universe is conspiring against us. He begins in verse 27 by reminding us that we are not on our own. Our ways are not hidden.[16] Though we may feel like we've been treated unjustly, God does not tire, nor does He cease His care for us. Everything that happens to us, God uses to either bless or discipline us. Which brings us back to our original question, "Why are you out of work?"

Isaiah 40 is addressed to a people who are in exile for not acknowledging God's authority. It might be tough to admit, but there are times when auditions might be hard to come by because we have lost sight of our calling. God's concern for His creation is shown by Him, "...not wishing for any to perish, but for all to come to repentance." (NASB)[17] His followers are a key component to bringing his plan about. In short, what jobs we have are secondary to the purpose God gives us. God will place His people where He needs them for maximum effectiveness. If, at some point, a Christian actor forgets why she has been given the opportunity to perform, it should not surprise her when God takes the opportunity away. I want to point out that it is an easy thing to forget that God is in charge of your career. Pride can make us feel solely responsible for our triumphs and defeats because God doesn't show up in the bad reviews or the applause. He's the silent partner, working feverishly behind our scenes.

Kind of like Sir Toby.

Following are two instances of people losing sight of why they were in the position God placed them. One is from the book of Daniel, and the other is a significant moment from my own experience. In Daniel 4, Nebuchadnezzar the king has had a dream about a great tree that is seen the whole world over. Then, a voice commands an angel to cut the tree down to a stump. The tree is promised a period of insanity, and the reason is given in the second half of verse 17:

> "...In order that the living may know
> That the Most High is ruler over the realm of mankind,
> And bestows it on whom He wishes
> And sets over it the lowliest of men."(NASB)[18]

It is Daniel's job to interpret the dream. He tells the king that the tree represents Nebuchadnezzar himself, and that heaven has decreed he should be cut down to size. Daniel also gives some hope to the king in verses 26 and27:

> "And in that it was commanded to leave the stump with the roots of the tree, your kingdom will be assured to you after you recognize that it is Heaven that rules. Therefore, O king, may my advice be pleasing to you: break away now from your sins by doing righteousness and from your iniquities by showing mercy to the poor, in case there may be a prolonging of your prosperity." [18]

Daniel tells Nebuchadnezzar, "...that it is Heaven that rules." If the king can recognize God's sovereignty before he goes crazy, then the prophecy can be averted. However, the next phrase in the text is, "All this happened to Nebuchadnezzar..." As he surveys the vastness of his kingdom, Nebuchadnezzar has a monologue about how powerful he must have been to gather together such a magnificent realm. Rarely do people listen to advice unless the speaker is their own experience. The king plunges into a horrifying madness described from verse 31 through 34. At the end of this episode in verse 34 is a turning point I hope all of us can come to:

> "But at the end of that period, I, Nebuchadnezzar, raised my eyes toward heaven and my reason returned to me, and I blessed the Most High and praised and honored Him who lives forever...(to verse 36b) And my majesty and splendor were restored to me for the glory of my kingdom, and my counselors and my nobles began seeking me out; so I was reestablished in my sovereignty, and surpassing greatness was added to me. Now I, Nebuchadnezzar, praise, exalt and honor the King of heaven, for all His works are true and His ways just, and He is able to humble those who walk in pride." (NASB) [18]

I see in this account the lengths to which God will go to get His people to be effective in their circles of influence. I had heard this story a number of times, but it never resonated with me like this until I went to graduate school. That was when my experience began to talk.

The University of San Diego offers an M.F.A. in performance. The program is connected with the Old Globe Theatres, and it is highly competitive. Less than 2% of the actors who audition make it in each year. Needless to say, once I was accepted, I felt pretty good about myself. Once every year, all of the actors in the program go through a professional review with the artistic staff of the Old Globe. At the time, Craig Noel, Richard Seer, and Jack O'Brien conducted the interview. I had been a good student, I worked hard, and I got along well with my classmates, so I expected something along the lines of, "Keep up the good work. We're glad to have you." What I got instead was a room of furrowed brows and tactful admonishment. They told me I was behind. I was uninteresting. I was inadequate for the work ahead.

I was shocked.

When I went home, I determined that what I needed to do was

train harder, work smarter, and be better. I was going to remind them why they accepted me. I was going to show them something new. I was going to make myself known.

I was so concerned with the "I" that I nearly went blind.

Thank God for inspiration. It suddenly occurred to me that I wasn't in grad school to become a better actor. There had to be some other divine purpose. What if I was specifically placed here to show this specific group of people who Jesus Christ is? It made perfect sense. I was spending over fourteen hours a day with the same seven class-mates. My campus was a Catholic university, and we were surrounded by the images of Christ. There were classes where we studied the in-fluence of the Christian God on the people in Shakespeare's day, and here I was completely forgetting the impact Christ had on me. My perspective shifted. I could empathize with Nebuchadnezzar when he said, "...my reason returned to me."(NASB)[18]

Once I removed my expectations from the professional acting program, and instead came to class and rehearsal each day to serve, things changed. I began playing larger roles. I began to have my voice heard. I began to get noticed. I became a much better performer. But none of that mattered to me (well, maybe it mattered a little...). The most rewarding moment of grad school came at the very end. After a very successful showcase in Los Angeles, the director of my grad pro-gram and I went for a walk. He was amazed at the progress I made and the performer I had become. It was as though, he said, I had become a different person. He was right. I was a different person, and I was able to lay out for him the spiritual journey that brought me there. It took my failure and God's intervention to allow me to share the gospel with one of the most respected people in my life.

Every time in my career, when I've felt responsible for getting work, the work has dried up. Every time I've submitted to God's will and said in my heart, "Here I am. Send me," the work has come. I have felt a kinship with Jonah in that respect. God will place us where He needs us when He needs us to be there. If we are unable to get our pride out of the way, He will either get someone else to do the job, or we will find ourselves on the sidelines until we get our heads right. We should be grateful when we are out of work that we aren't collecting unemployment checks from inside the belly of a fish. Are disobedience and pride the only reasons for the times of unemployment? Absolutely not, but they are prevalent, and they do create an ideal environment for fear to flourish. Regardless of the cause of unemployment, it offers us a chance for self-reflection and a firmer reliance on God's plan for us.

Psalm 90 sums up my prayer for you who are fearful in between jobs.

> Let Your work appear to Your servants
> And Your majesty to their children.
> Let the favor of the Lord our God be upon us;
> And confirm for us the work of our hands;
> Yes, confirm the work of our hands. (NASB)[19]

Do not be afraid.

DEVOTIONAL

1. Seek counsel regarding whether you are following God's direction or your own by choosing a career in performance. Tim Keller gives three criteria for finding your calling:

    a. Does the opportunity for the work continually come up?

    b. Do you have a passion for the work (not the applause)?

    c. Do you have a gift for the work? This one is tricky because it's a question you cannot answer alone. Others, who don't have a familial or friendly bias, have to see the gift.

2. Ask God to show you why you have been called into a life of performing.

3. How can God be honored in your career's current state?

CHAPTER 4

Inspiration

Art is a collaboration between God and the artist,
and the less the artist does the better.

– André Gide[1]

I don't know, I'm making this up as I go along.

– Indiana Jones[2]

When God Shows Up

I rolled out of bed and cleared my throat with a rumbly cough. Only, to my horror, I didn't clear my throat. Phlegm clung stubbornly in between the back of my throat and my soft palate. I hadn't taken a cold to bed, but apparently one had moved in while I was sleeping. I had been under a considerable amount of stress over the last few weeks. Graduate school was coming to a close, I was working on a few productions at the Old Globe, and my final project was due this evening. For our final semester our class was assigned to write, produce, and perform a one-man/one-woman show between 15 and 25 minutes in length. This project was to be the culmination of the work I had done over the last two and a half years. All of the faculty, the artistic staff from the Globe, and my family, who had travelled from out of state, would be there.

And at eight o'clock in the morning, I had no voice.

Flash forward to 7:30 p.m. The third project has begun, and I now have two voices. The one is the resonant, stuffy bass of your typical head cold, and the other is an awkward squeak. I had done everything in my power to bring back my voice, and nothing worked. All day long I called on God to help me, and He was silent. Then, I watched one of my classmates crash and burn. About seven minutes into his show, he got an enthusiastic response for something he wasn't expecting, and he blanked. You could see it in his face, then his shoulders. Soon, his whole body slumped as he grasped unsuccessfully for the next bit of dialogue. He managed to fumble through to the end, and he walked off stage and out the door without a word. I was next.

The first moment I opened my mouth, I was aware of another presence. My squeaky, clogged voice came out, and I knew God was with me. I had two characters in my piece, and I was playing both of them. The one thing I prayed so hard for God to take away turned out to be one of the best tools for differentiating these two people. One squawked, and the other rumbled, and I was on top until about the seven minute mark.

At that moment my memory went blank. I know it was the seven minute mark because I could see in my mind where I was at the bottom of the third page, but I couldn't see anything on page four. Instead of panic, however, I felt a warm covering of peace. It may sound incredible, but at that moment, I heard God's voice in my soul. This is what He said:

"My grace is sufficient for you, for my power is made perfect in weakness." (NASB)[3]

Or, how I actually heard it:

"Follow Me. I got this one."

In the time it took to inhale, He showed me my day. I saw how He'd carried me through every moment. My cold was from Him. My family's and faculty's support was from Him. Even this moment of freefall was from Him. I believe He did all of this to show me Himself, and to draw me closer to Him. For the remainder of the show, I had absolutely no clue what my next lines were going to be, but I knew, *I knew*, God would not only give me the words to speak, but He'd tell me how to say them. It was the first moment of my life that I was conscious of working side-by-side with God as His servant. I never thought it would happen on stage, and the experience changed me forever.

Who's Got It?

Over the last several years, I have come to realize what happened to me that evening in San Diego was not a performance, but worship. In C.S. Lewis' *Reflections on the Psalms*, he says, "It is in the process of being worshipped that God communicates His presence to men."[4] In this light, worship and inspiration would seem to have an intimate connection.

Inspiration gets called a number of different names in the theatre. Some call it instinct. Some call it the muse. Some of the more "spiritual" actors call it simply, the universe. Stanislavski called it the subconscious. Whatever its name, it is regarded as the magical elixir of creativity. Some people seem to have loads of it while others flounder. It also ebbs and flows with little regard for whom it lands on. Each time the concept is invoked, it carries a vague sense of divine benevolence. For the Christian, inspiration should hold a little less ambiguity. We should be familiar with the concept from the Bible's use of it. The word, "inspire", shows up in the 12th century and means, "to breathe life into,"[5] something. We see it for the first time when God literally breathes life into Adam's dusty nostrils. Again, in the New Testament, the Bible claims to be "God breathed,"(NASB).[6] Inspiration meets the theatre when character, actor, audience, and show come together in what can only be called a perfect moment. Actors live for these moments, and the desire for consistently inspired performances has given seed to the various acting methods and techniques found in the theatre today.

Artists have long pondered how to harness the power of the creative energy of God. Some pray. Some drink. Some buy books looking for answers. However, the creative power of God cannot be harnessed. The syllogism that all good things come from God, therefore, only people who have pleased God can be inspired, proves false over time. There is no formula, or ritual, or level of devotion capable of forcing God to divulge His secrets. This is evidenced by the panoply of artists who have produced so many great works over the centuries. It doesn't take long to find inspired art crafted by artists who not only claim to be atheists, but openly attack Christianity. I state this, not to degrade the worth of art created by people who do not worship the Christian God; rather, I want to point out that Christians do not have a monopoly on God's moving voice. The Bible is clear regarding the seemingly capricious nature of God's favor. Matthew 5:45 states:

> "... for He causes His sun to rise on the evil and the good, and
> sends rain on the righteous and the unrighteous." (NASB)[7]

We are also given ample examples of God speaking to, and through, all manner of people. Pharaoh and Nebuchadnezzar had dreams, Samuel was only a child when God spoke to him, and Balaam and his donkey both end up speaking words God gave them.

THE ACTOR'S HOMEWORK

1. Evaluate yourself on how much you listen to your "instincts." Do your peers and directors say you are in your head too much?

2. In your opinion, how much should an actor rely on his gut versus his research?

3. How do you physically/mentally/spiritually prepare yourself for inspiration before rehearsals and performance?

Giving Up (control)

It is difficult for some Christians when God's purposes and plans do not align themselves with human concepts of justice or reciprocity. In Peter Shaffer's play, *Amadeus*, Salieri declares war on God because his piety isn't rewarded, and the hedonistic Mozart is producing vast quantities of divine music as though, "...taking dictation." Finally, when Salieri has had enough, he erupts, "They say the breath of God bloweth where it listeth, but I say it should list to virtue, or it should not blow at all!"[8] Salieri is made a villain in this play, but he's a sympathetic one. Most of us like to believe that the better we are as people, the more God will make us successful. Whole churches are built around the concept of good living as a program for God's favor, but the economy of grace described in the Bible does not work this way. God's grace depends on an action already completed (the life, death, and resurrection of Jesus) to produce a fundamentally changed humanity. This new humanity then works for the preservation and betterment of the world through a sense joy and hope instead of a sense of entitlement or fear.

Humans are adverse to the Biblical economy because it is fundamentally antithetical to the human economy. We work, or we don't get paid. We treat those in power with respect, and we expect some recognition or promotion. However, the idea of coming up with a "deal" with God where each party gives the other something they need infers an equality between the Creator of the universe and His creation that doesn't exist. This should make us grateful. Only a God who is capable of guiding, challenging, and using us is worth worshiping. Developing empathy and overcoming fear both require a bit of effort on behalf of the actor. Inspiration, however, remains unique because the performer is, by definition, not responsible for it in any way.

How then do we learn to take hold and use something that cannot be controlled? The answer lies in the concept of surrender. Given the seeming randomness of inspiration, and the character of God as described in the Bible, I propose that inspiration (God's prompting) is a constant influence in the lives of all people. He is constantly talking to His creation. Romans 1 tells us God's invisible qualities, His divine nature and eternal power have been clearly seen in His creation since time began.[9] Some people are simply better at hearing it than others. It is not then, a matter of being lucky enough to be selected by God, but rather a discipline of being able to pick out God's voice amongst all the other white noise of the world. However, merely noticing God's influence is not enough. The Christian actor should strive to act on divine impulse, and over time she will be able to give her entire performance into God's hands. It is the difference between *using* something and being used *by* something.

Discerning God's Voice

Responding to inspiration consists of two actions: listening and obeying. The Christian actor should be able to discern between inspiration and her own motivations. The first, and most important step in separating the two comes down to belief. The actor is called to believe in the given circumstances of her character, and the Christian is called to believe in the given circumstances of her faith. The actor playing Hamlet must accept a number of things: his father's ghost is both real and telling the truth, Ophelia is in love with him, a person who dies without last rites is doomed to hell, and a person killed after (or even during) confession is taken into heaven. Likewise, a Christian has to accept God's existence, God's sovereignty, God's power, and God's personal care for His creation. The only difference between the actor and the Christian then is what is at stake. For Hamlet, it's an imaginary Denmark. For the Christian, it's the fate of the universe, and for Christians it just so happens to be "for real." Just as much as a play's given circumstances affect the life of the character, the given circumstances outlined in the Bible should affect the life of the Christian actor.

If an actor claims to believe in God, the best way to understand the character of God is through the Bible. With a thorough, ongoing study of God's word, a cycle begins. First, God's voice and character become easier to distinguish. The more we know about the character of God, the more we see the difference between His will and the world's. The more we understand His will for creation, the more we see His concern for us on a personal level. Over time, that concern generates trust as we see God's promises in action both in Scripture and our daily lives. Finally, trust enables us to both hear God's voice during the maelstrom of performance, and then act upon the impulses He gives us. In a very real way, inspiration is direct communion with God, and it starts with the Bible.

Until I was in graduate school, Biblical study always fell into the category of things I knew I should do, along with things like praying and flossing. However, it was never a priority for me. There were parts of the Bible I didn't understand, and there were parts of it that I didn't want to understand. It was a lot like reading Shakespeare, and, at the time, that wasn't a good thing. Thankfully, times change. I knew when I entered grad school that I would have to confront my fear of the Bard. What I didn't know was how a poet who lived nearly 450 years ago could be the lynchpin to my discovery of the Bible.

I was spending hours with plays like *Julius Caesar* and *Twelfth Night*, memorizing passages, defining words, discovering the characters and their motivations. Eventually, I found I could quote many of the plays at will, and because of the tremendous human insight in the writing, many of these quotes could apply to whatever situation I happen to be in. As God was moving in my life, I realized that I was treating the plays like I should have been treating the Bible. I also found that the very same tools I had been given in my Shakespeare class could be used to understand God's Word. In order to stay on topic, I outlined in detail the method and tools I used for Bible study in the chapter entitled: "The Toolbox". The point is, had I not spent time studying God's word, I would never have been able to recognize God's voice during my one person show, and I could have easily slumped my shoulders and given up.

DEVOTIONAL

1. Hearing God's voice may sound a little strange. Psalm 139:23-24 is an invitation for God to search the psalmist and know him. Invite God to do the same as a regular part of your daily conversations with God. In doing so, God doesn't usually keep silent. This is a great way to begin listening to God's voice and movement in your life.

2. Reflect upon a time where you felt God's leading either on stage or off.

    a. What was your response?

    b. What was the response of the people around you?

3. How often do you operate under the human economy (I give therefore I get) versus the economy of grace (I don't deserve, but yet I get)?

Practical Inspiration

Going back to the definition of inspiration and breathing life into something, it would be good to tackle a fundamental of performance many beginning actors struggle with. I have sat through (maybe suffered is a better word) a number of auditions/monologues/scenes that have no life. The actors have all of their lines down, their bodies are moving, even their faces show me they know and believe what they are saying, but there is no spark. The reason for this occurred to me while shooting a television pilot.

The actor we had cast to play the father came in unprepared. He asked if we could hide the lines somewhere off camera, and because we were already thick into production with no time or money to spare, we let him get away with it. At first, it seemed to work. I didn't see him looking directly at the lines, but there was something intangibly wrong. It was as though the actor had become an energy vortex, sucking the life out everything around him, including the scenery. After several takes I saw the source of the void. As soon as the director of photography said, "Rolling," the actor would take a second to exhale all of his air. By the time he heard, "Action," there was just a fraction of the oxygen in his lungs necessary to sustain life, let alone deliver his lines.

I do not know where the practice started, but I see young actors do the same thing all of the time. They'll step on stage, put their heads down, shake their arms, forcefully blow out all the air in their bodies... and NOT BREATHE IN. Just like God breathes life and thought into people, actors have to breathe life into their characters, a function they cannot do unless...THEY BREATHE IN. While I was watching the actor in our pilot, I was reminded of the phrase acting for the camera teachers use: *You can always tell on screen when someone is thinking.* Our actor was saying his lines, moving where we told him to go, but his eyes were blank; there was no discernible thought happening on camera. I saw in his performance, and in the performance of some of my beginning students, the symbiotic connection between breath and thought.

Listen to the people around you talk. They will rarely run out of breath. Why? There are a number of things that happen before sounds come out of a person's mouth. First, she is stimulated by something. Second, the person will come up with the gist of what they want to say. The gist is then filtered through the given circumstances of the person talking and whatever given circumstances the talking person knows about the listener. Then words come out. Even while words are spilling out of people, the editing and revising process continues in the form of appositives, restatements, and stutters, most of which are done in a single breath, hence the argument that the breath connects the thought to speech and action.

On stage, all of the thought about what actors have to say and to whom they should say it has been done for them. What happens then, is an actor subconsciously skips a lot of the processes required for speaking. The stimuli for speaking changes from something another person has said or done to a silence that needs to be filled with the next line. The line must then be said, but because the actor hasn't formulated the thought for himself, he will often run out of breath before the line ends (Thank you Mr. Shakespeare and Mr. Shaw for long thoughts).

Even though the thinking of the actor has been taken care of with regard to what he is going to say, it must appear as though what is being said and what is happening on the stage is happening for the first time.[10] Not only does the actor have to go through all of the processes of thought required before speech, but the audience has to feel her do it as well. That means the actor must find within the speeches and actions in the play the *reasons* for her character to speak and move himself. Once those reasons are found and highlighted, the actor must practice inhaling (or inspiring) at those spots. The inhale should happen at the precise moment of the stimuli. Be aware that there may be multiple times a character will be prompted to say something before she is able to get a word in. Breathe in these places as well. You will find these added breaths will do wonders for spurring your scene partners to say their lines with urgency and conviction. Changing the way you highlight your script will show you where to breathe. Score your script with a highlighter and a pencil. Use the highlighter to mark your cue lines, and the pencil to mark when your character is inspired to speak or move. This trigger is where you will breathe. Below is an example of what a script should look like. We will assume the part of Randy:

(Randy and Cooper are 30-something males. Randy has come to Cooper's house to be there for his friend after a tough breakup. Tough breakups are a specialty of Cooper's. Cooper lives in an ultra-modern house overlooking Westwood California. It is after midnight, and Cooper is waiting by his pool for Randy to arrive.)

(Randy enters from the gate)

> **Randy will breathe on his entrance. All movement should be considered the same as thought. Movement is merely a silent tactic in the scene to accomplish a character's objective.**

RANDY: I thought you'd be inside.

COOPER: It's too cold inside.

> **Randy's next line is a topic or beat change. I am going to assume he is polite enough to listen to his friend. If I were making the choice to be impolite because the stakes of the scene demanded it, I would mark the breath at the beginning of the line at "It's."**

RANDY: So what happened?

COOPER: What?

Cooper's evasion will cause Randy to jump in as soon as possible. Breathing on the line prior to yours cuts out the dead space in the dialogue.

RANDY: What did you do this time?

COOPER: Nothing. She went crazy on me. Completely insane.

There are two breaths because Randy has two thoughts. The first thought never gets voiced (but the audience can fill it in). The second thought is the line Randy delivers below. Randy won't stand for "Nothing" as an answer. When Randy breathes here, Cooper has to counter with an excuse. These chances to breathe within your partner's lines give a realism and a life to a scene.

RANDY: Wow. She never struck me as the crazy type.

I am a firm believer in letting the audience see and hear the actor breathe. In stage combat, there is a step called the "cue." This is a moment where the audience and the punch-ee get to see the punch-er's fist, frozen in time for one second, right before it lays him out. The cue draws focus to the action about to happen. An inhalation will do the same thing for dialogue. It tells the audience, "Hey, look over here. A line is about to be said." Two actors, breathing in each other's lines, giving and taking focus with their eyes and their breath can make any scene feel like it is happening for the first time.

THE ACTOR'S HOMEWORK

1. Use the script scoring exercise from the previous chapter to add in when your character breathes.

Breath: A Secondary Function

Breath has another function within a scene. The Stanislavski system was developed in order to create believable responses to manufactured stimuli. In order to do this, actors had to become students of their emotions, taking a mental inventory of their bodies when their emotions changed. Stanislavski theorized that all incoming stimuli caused a physical reaction, however slight, and if the actor could somehow reconstruct the physical response, the accompanying emotion would then follow suit[10]. It was like reverse engineering applied to grief or joy. His theories proved sound, and his method of physical actions have been a staple in acting schools across the world ever since. Underlying Stanislavski's method is where breath comes in.

There is a pattern to physical and emotional reactions. First comes the stimulus, then the breath, and finally the reaction. Breath is a gateway for the stimulus to allow emotions to emerge. When upset, a person will often hold her breath in order to avoid breaking down. When the emotion is too powerful to contain, the breath will then change in order to let the body feel the sensations the stimuli caused. This is why sobs occur. A held breath is let out in violent bursts because the emotion is so great. In much the same way, the method of physical actions creates authentic emotions (without the psychological damage of re-hashing past traumas). If an actor is able to recreate the breathing patterns she experiences during an emotion, she is able to tap into that emotion more easily. In fact, breath is necessary for the actor to truly recreate the physicality of an emotion. Character development must go so deep it causes the actor to actually breathe in character.

The key to both divine and practical inspiration is practice. Many actors will brag about "winging" it when they go on stage, but relying on inspiration is a different discipline. If an actor wants to really hear God's leading, she has to accustom herself to getting her own agenda out of the way, and that takes time and grace. If she wants to use her breath to add life to a scene or depth to an emotion, her instrument has to be ready to both hear and respond to whatever stimuli her scene partner dishes out. Over time, surrendering to inspiration may begin to feel easy, so it is important for the actor, in order to maintain a humble spirit, to remind both herself and her colleagues Who is really calling the shots.

CHAPTER 5

Work Ethic

"I love deadlines. I like the whooshing sound they make as they fly by."

– Douglas Adams[1]

"For even when we were with you, we used to give you this order:
if anyone is not willing to work, then he is not to eat, either.
For we hear that some among you are leading an undisciplined life,
doing no work at all, but acting like busybodies."

– The Apostle Paul[2]

The Odds

According to a 2012 article by Brendan McMahon in the Huffington Post titled: "Unemployment, A Lifestyle for Actors," the unemployment rate among actors who are members of Actor's Equity (the professional union for stage actors) is 90%.[3] This is the fact many acting teachers use on the first day of class to "cull the herd." While

I don't agree with the tactic, I find it hard to argue with the statistic. Actors need to consider that the overwhelming majority of the people who practice their profession are unemployed, but it doesn't have to scare them away. I think the reason most actors aren't working is… most actors aren't working. Allow me to explain.

Statistics can be frightening, but in reality they are just tools. Businesses use stats to formulate effective plans. Since actors also function as small businesses, they can use stats in the same way. So, what does that 90% actually represent?

The 90% represents all of the people who pay dues to the Actors' Equity Association. AEA is comprised of actors and stage managers of all ages, and entrance is permitted after gaining employment in AEA endorsed theatrical productions. Becoming an equity member is a costly endeavor, and it can take a couple of years to qualify. It would make sense that anyone who had spent that much effort to join Equity would have a greater drive to cultivate her career, but that isn't always the case. A small minority of Equity members hold on to their cards because it represents a lot of work, and the annual dues aren't enough to convince them to drop it. Others, and I would say a vast majority, would consider themselves active members, but are not pursuing performance work as efficiently or aggressively as they should. The point is, there are a lot of actors in the marketplace, but not all of them should be considered serious competition for the diligent performer. The question then becomes, how does an actor make her way into the 10% of the people in the profession who *have* found work?

Many schools do a decent job of training an actor to do her job. What is missing, though, is any sort of direction regarding how to get that job. One of the biggest complaints I hear from actors who aren't working (whether it's professional, community, or educational theatre, the complaint is the same) is that the same people are always getting cast. This seems dreadfully unfair to them, but I venture to say they wouldn't mind so much if they were part of the "same people." This means, there is a small community of performers who have "figured it out." What have they learned that the other 90% have not? Going into this profession, it is necessary to meet an ugly truth head on. The entertainment industry is built on nepotism.

Take some time to let that sink in.

Now, instead of railing against the world for keeping you out of their tea party, consider why this is the case. If you had a choice between doing what you love with strangers or doing what you love with people you trust and respect, which would you choose? Many performers have dreamed of starting their own company, so they can produce their own work with their own people. The dream can become a reality with a certain amount of initiative. The proactive performer won't throw her hands up in the air and cry foul, she will either A) produce her own work, or B) use her time and effort to figure out how to become one of the 10%. It won't take long to discover that the common thread binding the "always cast" together is relationship. Look at movie directors like Wes Anderson, Joss Whedon, Tim Burton, and Christopher Nolan. They have developed an ensemble of performers, a group of creative minds who understand one another. An ensemble is a powerful creative force, and a good director works hard to create one. What a new actor on the outside of an ensemble has difficulty grasping is that an ensemble is not an inaccessible group. To join, an actor must first develop a relationship, and relationships take respect, consistency, and time to cultivate. Respect comes from being seen in action. Consistency is the result of disciplined performance, and time is the oven in which the relationship is cooked. Understanding these principles and how they develop is crucial for building a long-term career.

Being Seen: Film

When an actor starts her career, especially in a new city, a vicious circle seems to swirl in front of her. She can't get work because no one knows her, but how is anyone to get to know her if she can't get work?

In the past, getting an industry professional to see her work meant she had to navigate her way passed agents and casting directors to book a role and get lucky enough to have the project screen at a reputable festival. If she had found work, piecing together a reel was an arduous and skill-heavy task. Now, with the rapid development of camera and computer technology, it has never been easier to create, edit, and display her own content. Websites like youtube.com, funnyordie.com, or even vimeo.com offer a free venue for film actors to showcase their work. However, with the relative ease of creating and posting a video online, the internet is now swamped with material. The new problem then is directing someone to her content. The best ways to do that are the subject of a far larger book, or a graduate level marketing course, but there are some general rules of thumb:

- *Maintain a high level of quality:* Protect your online body of work by only posting what you want to be seen by the general public. Avoid videos with poor image and sound quality. You may have loved that play at the community center, but that video captured by your aunt's iphone from the back row probably doesn't catch the majesty of the actual performance. Also, take down those audition pieces for projects that have passed.

- *Keep it short:* Even if you've done a feature length piece, keep the clips you post under two to three minutes, maximum. If you want people to see more, supply them with links to other short clips.

- *Funny wins:* There is a hierarchy to what people will surf the internet to watch. Funny beats drama every time. If you have good dramatic work, put it on your website and direct traffic to them from your funnier work on sites like youtube.com. If people are interested enough to visit your site, they will have no problem watching some longer, more dramatic work while they're there.

At the very least, an actor pursuing a career in film needs to make something called a reel. A reel is a sort of commercial for an actor's product. It should be clean, fast, fun, and tell anyone who sees it exactly who this actor thinks she is. Like headshots, a professional reel can be costly. However, there is a lot of software out there that makes putting together an amateur reel both simple and cost effective. Where does someone collect footage for her reel? An actor just starting out in the film and television world needs to be auditioning or creating her own content all the time. The more footage she gets, the more chances she has finding the perfect shot. The footage can come from any project; student or independent films should not be underestimated. The right camera, the right light, the right angle, or even the right line is all it takes to build ninety seconds of material, showcasing what she does best.

Being Seen: Theatre

For theatre, the process of being seen is a little different. Creating and producing a short film has far fewer steps than producing a piece of theatre. Theatre actors, therefore, use four main strategies to market themselves to industry professionals: mail campaigns, referrals, open audition calls or classes, and the last is getting the agent/casting director to see them in a production. Each method has its advantages, but some are more effective than others.

Many actors will come into a new city and flood the agent and casting markets with headshots and resumes. Though this method does get the actor's picture and work history in front of a wide variety of people, there needs to be something impressive about one or the other in order to draw anyone's attention. A recognizable production of a successful show, a credible theatre, a rigorous training program, or a respected director or producer on a resume can all catch the attention of the reviewer. All of these credits, however, are second-hand relationships for the agents and casting directors, and it is burdensome to trust these relationships enough to bring an actor in. Considering the expense of mass mail, coupled with the relatively low positive return, make mailing three hundred headshots and resumes a waste of time and money. Mail campaigns have merit, but they work best when used in conjunction with some of the other strategies listed below. For a terrific way to approach mailing agents, read *Acting as a Business* by Brian O'Neil.[4]

Getting a meeting with an agent is no small task, so actors should do whatever they can to book one. The theatre community is often fairly tight-knit, and performers are usually willing to help each other out. If an actor knows someone who has a relationship with a casting director or an agent, then the actor can ask her friend to set up a meeting. The more respectable the referral, the more likely a meeting will be arranged. In the case of a referral, though, she must realize the agent is meeting with her as a favor to a mutual friend. Therefore, an actor's main objective in an interview should not be to impress, but to develop her own relationship with the agent. Once a relationship has been established, then both parties can consider whether they want to work together or not.

Auditions are the least expensive way to showcase talent (if an audition ever has a fee attached, it's a good sign whoever is running the interview is a crook). In major theatre markets like New York or Los Angeles there are many opportunities to audition for important industry people. Finding audition opportunities is much easier than most new actors think, but it takes initiative. The first place to look for projects run by reputable casting directors is the AEA website (actorsequity.org), under the "Casting Call" link. Another (semi) free resource for finding auditions are websites like actorsaccess.com, nowcasting.com, or castingnetworks.com. Membership to these websites are free, but there is a fee to access some of the more useful functions. The Drama Book Shop (dramabookshop.com) sells a monthly publication called *The Season Overview*, which lists auditions and season information for all of the regional theatres in the country. Industry publications like *Backstage* (west or east) and *Variety* also have audition notices, but they each charge a subscription fee. Auditions can also be found on their online counterparts: backstage.com or variety.com, respectively. Lastly, most cities will have a casting website or hotline of some kind, and there is also something to be said about walking in the front doors of a theatre and asking when and where auditions are held. Granted, auditions apply more to getting in front of casting directors than agents, but being seen is being seen. Entering an agent's office with a casting director's referral is a great way to add credibility for an actor.

Similar to auditions, there are also a number of "classes" actors can take that boast agents and casting directors as instructors. Classes may be too strong a word for some of these pay-to-play opportunities, but there are some studios who really do try to teach their students something useful. Look for studios who audition actors before enrollment. Studios who are selective about their clientele draw a much higher level of casting director and agent. The classes are usually geared toward cold reading skills. Actors are given new material, a scene partner, and maybe ten minutes to work the piece. Everyone gets a turn, and if the actor is lucky, the instructor will work the scene. Typically though, the night turns out to be more of a chance to perform in front of a casting director in a low stress environment. Casting directors have as much of a type as actors do, so actors should research the types of theatres or films the casting director has represented before paying for a chance to be seen.

Finally, the theatre actor can invite agents and casting directors to watch her perform in a showcase or a production. Showcases are usually one-night performances of a series of scenes or one-act plays, specifically tailored to highlight the performer's strengths. A good actor training program will offer a showcase after graduation, and the quality of the program is often directly reflected in the success of its showcase. Whether the program turns out famous people is less important than whether their actors find representation right after graduation. There are also independent showcases produced by a group of actors who want to be seen. These are harder to get industry professionals to come to because the depth of talent varies widely. Even if the all of the actors are incredibly talented, casting directors and agents don't know that, and the attendance at independent showcases is typically low. Therefore, the best case scenario for an actor to be seen is to invite an agent to a recognizable, reputable theatre's production. Typically, there will be someone in the cast who is already represented, so an actor should target agencies represented in the cast. If an actor is seen doing wonderful work, she will have earned respect for her talent. This puts the actor in a new and advantageous position. Instead of hunting down people in the industry, the industry will look for her. Even if the actor isn't contacted immediately after the show, the stage is now set for the her to request a meeting with an agent who is now familiar with her work.

Discipline

Despite the long investment in developing a reputation for hard work and integrity, it is by far the most reliable way to ensure an actor's career. If respect for an actor's talent is a way of getting a job, a good work ethic is a way of keeping one (and getting more). Anyone can get hired anywhere once, but it takes a certain quality to be invited back to a theatre. As a director, when I get an actor's resume I often look for repeated credits. Variety is important, but I like when an actor has already earned another theatre's respect for her work ethic. I have cast an actor who works hard over a talented actor many times, simply because I know the amount (and type) of work I can expect. The trick to establishing a good reputation can be summed up in one word: discipline.

Discipline is an interesting quality. I have heard people say, "I'm just not disciplined." However, what I think they are really saying is, "I'm not disciplined in the areas I need/should/want to be." I'm not sure anyone is naturally disciplined because discipline is only required when we need to accomplish worthwhile tasks that challenge us. For example, I have friends who love to run. They run all the time, and there is something wrong in their brains telling them they are having fun. My wife hates to run, but she gets up with the sun three times each week to put her miles in. My wife has disciplined herself to do what she doesn't enjoy because she believes the end result is worth it. Let us say an actor needs to assign tactics to every beat of her script. If she enjoys this type of puzzle solving, she will easily move things around in her life to do it. It's fun. If she doesn't like slogging through the paperwork of character development, she will find other, more desirable activities – unless she's disciplined. In short, it isn't the type of work, it's the heart of the actor that determines whether something requires discipline or not. If actors need to compete with their bodies, voices, spirits, and brains, chances are they are going to need some form of discipline in one or more of these areas in order to succeed.

As stated elsewhere in the book, the body is the actor's most precious asset, which also means it can be a huge liability if the actor is undisciplined about maintaining her health. Throughout training, an actor learns several ways to keep her body in a limber state of relaxed readiness. Often, she will learn exercises in class to gain control of her body, but she won't practice them outside of class. She won't progress at the rate she needs to in order to compete in the professional arena. Exercises, by definition, are designed to be used over time in order to get the actor into shape. Actors should develop a training regimen, or incorporate the body work learned in class into their pre-existing workout routine. There is a sample body exercise in the appendix for this chapter.

The body can also be a liability when the actor shows up to rehearsal, and her body isn't ready to perform. Perform is a key word here. Actors must learn that performance begins long before opening night. Each chance an actor gets to use her skills is a chance to perform. Her body needs to be ready for rehearsals and auditions in the same way she readies it for a paying audience. Cast warmups for rehearsals are a privilege of educational theatre. In the professional world, the actor is expected to show up ready to perform the first minute of rehearsal. This means an actor's real call time needs to allow for an individual body warmup. The same concept applies to auditions. Many actors work another job. They have to squeeze in an audition on a break, and they don't allow time to engage their bodies beforehand. Having been on the casting side of the table for some time, I can immediately tell an actor whose body is her ally and an actor whose body isn't even awake. Unfortunately, the audition is the first place casting directors get a glimpse of an actor's work ethic. Because the body is the gateway for the audience into the world of the play, it needs to be the most prepared to be in the scene. If an actor places all of her prep time for an audition on given circumstances and how she will say her lines, but neglects to get her body into the scene, most of her work will be a waste. Taking a yoga class, or hiring a private teacher who knows Alexander technique are great ways for the undisciplined actor to keep her body under her command and build a support group to keep her accountable.

The actor's voice is also incredibly important to keep in top shape. Granted, musical theatre performers must continue studying privately throughout their careers, but what is there to do for an actor who doesn't sing? Just like the body, being disciplined about the voice is a mixture of keeping it healthy and keeping it limber.

Vocal health is fragile, and the serious actor should consider everything that passes through her esophagus before putting it into her body. Obviously, smoking is damaging to the instrument, regardless of the substance inside the paper, but there are a few other things to avoid to keep the voice healthy. Stay away from any substances that dry out the throat, like caffeine, sugar, or alcohol. Does this mean an actor cannot enjoy a drink with the cast after a show? It might. This is where discipline comes in. When everyone is outside for a smoke break, it is difficult to keep from lighting up, but every decision about every substance put into the body needs to become a decision about strengthening or weakening the instrument. The focus that comes through discipline is an edge for an actor, and actors should be looking for any edge they can get.

Integral to sustaining vocal health is vocal exercise. A healthy voice is great, but it also needs strength, range, and dexterity in order to affect other actors and an audience in performance. Thinking of the voice in these three categories make it easier for an actor to determine strengths and weaknesses, and she can work them according to their need. The more control the actor has over these three areas, the more of an edge she has when she is considered for a role.

The voice should be trained like a gymnast rather than a linebacker. Strength (or volume) is required for both sustainability and power. Thinking of volume in terms of strength helps keep the voice healthy, especially while working emotional scenes. Musicians use the same concept. Instead of using "loud," they use the Italian word, "forte." Strength in the voice is developed by working the mechanisms for breathing and resonating. Lung capacity and diaphragm strength are the gas tanks and the power plant (respectively) for vocal production. Just like working the body, exercises need to be done with regularity and an intensity of focus, or the muscles will atrophy. Unlike other muscles in the body, though, atrophy in the voice won't be visible, so loss of power will not be noticeable until the power is needed (but unavailable).

Pitch variation adds flavor, and the more range an actor has, the more options she has in character development. The lungs and diaphragm are fairly large apparatuses within the human body. The vocal folds, on the other hand are quite small, but they are still muscles. The types of exercises for vocal range will be familiar to anyone studying private voice, and they must also be practiced with some regularity. Since it is easy to damage a voice, and since vocal damage takes a significant time to heal, the importance of a trained, expert ear, who can guide the actor in her growth cannot be overestimated.

Lastly, vocal dexterity is needed for articulation and clarity. After strong airflow has been generated and it passes through the vocal folds, only then can the sounds be formed into words. This is the work of the articulators: the tongue, the lips, and the teeth. Conditioning the articulators enable the actor to be understood, and it opens up the ability to adopt dialects and speech patterns. Actors who attempt dialect work without a firm foundation in vocal dexterity will find it difficult to sustain non-native sounds for the duration of a production with any consistency. Again, it comes back to exercise to ensure the actor's teeth, tongue, and lips are ready for the verbal gymnastics the great plays of the world have to offer.

All three vocal areas (strength, range, and dexterity) are easy to take for granted. Most of us have been talking for a good part of our lives, and we seem to get by in our everyday world. The theatre, however, demands more. We don't go to the theatre to see ordinary people behaving in ordinary ways in ordinary circumstances. We go to the theatre to experience the transformation of the ordinary into the extraordinary. Much like Jesus takes completely mundane objects like bread and wine and makes them holy, or God takes the broken, the inadequate, and the fallen of this world and makes them His champions, the theatre transforms characters to be more than what they seem, forcing them to explore the heights and depths of their ability to express themselves. An actor must rise to that challenge, and her voice shouldn't hold her back.

THE ACTOR'S HOMEWORK

1. Identify the area(s) in which you lack discipline (Body, Voice, Spirit, Brain).

2. Develop a plan to engage your area of weakness. Write it down. Ask for someone to come along beside you as an accountability partner.

3. Using the exercises in this book as a starting point, develop a warmup of your own for each of the areas (Body, Voice, Spirit, Brain).

The Big Problem

At the end of the book there are several physical and vocal exercises designed to get the actor's body and voice in shape to compete in the marketplace. They are tools, and, like tools, are only useful if they come out of the tool box. When actors are performing eight shows a week while traveling around the country, exercise and rest need to be scheduled into their day; otherwise, they are likely to get missed. Knowing this, the actor should get in the habit now of scheduling when to work out her instruments and when to rest them. The breakdown for many performers who seem to have trouble being disciplined about the sort of work outlined above, is that they cannot see the value. They either can't see how much better off their instrument will be if they work on it, or they are convinced their instrument is desirable enough (and therefore doesn't need any work). Both are deceived. In a way, it's much like how many Christians live out their faith. The exercises mentioned in the book parallel the spiritual disciplines of regularly meeting with other believers, self reflection, and private Bible study. Without them, the Christian cannot hope to grow into the woman God desires her to be. The biggest difference between the undisciplined actor and the undisciplined Christian is that nothing happens to the undisciplined actor. She simply stops acting. The Christian, however, who does not discipline herself will find herself disciplined by God. This premise leaves the Christian performer in a precarious position. If she is called by God to a career in the theatre, she must be disciplined in both her vocation and her spiritual life. The apostle Paul tells us that we need to work as though working for God.[5] God uses our work ethic as a light to both our fellow actors and audiences.

I can understand the man who has to dig deep to give his best as he pushes papers around an office. I can see how the man who works his body to the bone with hard labor would long for a break. I can empathize with the man who forces himself out of bed to get to a job that saps his soul. What I cannot understand are actors with a poor work ethic. Actors eat, sleep, and dream about the day they finally find work. There are so many times in a performer's life where there isn't work that working hard when the work comes should be a natural response. In practice, though, many actors are guilty of laziness. Fortunately, the further up the professional ladder we climb, the more lazy actors seem to get weeded out.

The Christian performer has no excuse for laziness. The Bible is full of examples and exhortations for a good work ethic, but somehow the acting world is full of men and women, both Christian and not, who don't do "the work." Looking critically and empathically, I can see three causes for a broken work ethic in the entertainment industry. Some people choose to be actors because it looks easy. After all, how hard can it be to fly to exotic locations, wear expensive clothes, and memorize a few words here and there? The life of an actor is many things, but a life of ease is not one of them. Others are not sure of what the work of acting really is. For most people with jobs, there is a building where the work happens, and the work can be left there at the end of the day. Production is different. Rehearsals are meant for discovery and play, so most of the actor's work must take place outside of rehearsals and shooting. On set, artists will bring a menu from which the director will choose what she likes best. Lastly, and most tragically, some actors don't know what is at stake. It is difficult for a lot of performers to think any further ahead than the next audition, much less a year, or five years, or eternity. Thus, there is a huge population of actors out there waiting for the phone to ring, wondering why they're not famous.

This section may seem obvious to you because I don't think the group of people I'm addressing would have gotten this far in the book. Laziness knows no bounds. There are just as many performers in the professional world as there are in the worlds of community theatre and independent film. The men and women who, after a grueling day at the office arrive at the theatre in the strip mall, put on the costumes they've sewn themselves, walk out on to the sets they have built, and play under the lights they have hung, are the some of the hardest working people in the business. It is not lesser work; it's just harder, and I believe the difficulty is a large part of what brings these dentists, waitresses, and plumbers together. There are "others" though, who avoid the difficult bits of the work but indulge in the perks that come with a life in the theatre. Sonia Moore captures Stanislavski's thoughts about the "other" when she records his words, "*Others* love not art itself but an actor's career, success; they revive in the backstage atmosphere...the others are abominable...The habit of being always in public, of exhibiting oneself and showing off, of receiving applause, good reviews, and so on, is a great temptation; it accustoms an actor to being worshiped; it spoils him."[6]

I see this "other" all the time at the university level. Typically, they are the breed of performer who have no trouble showing up on time to rehearsal if they have a decent role. They have no problem showing up for the performance, but you won't see them at strike. They are the same actors who, when asked about their career, might say, "I'll keep performing until it isn't fun anymore." This phrase is common among performers. I've even said it, but I've come to realize that it revealed in me a selfishness that poisoned my art. Many of us enjoy acting. There is, admittedly, a large amount of play involved. However, there are times when it is work, and it is everything you can do to maintain a positive attitude. At times like this, even the best of us can be tempted to be a little self-centered. As discussed elsewhere in this book, a self-centered approach to art is a limiting approach.

Self-indulgence is only one type of laziness. The more insidious type of laziness is what the Bible is talking about in Proverbs, when it talks of, "A little sleep, a little slumber, a little folding of the hands to rest –"[7] If an actor isn't careful, much of her life will be spent waiting for something to happen. I see more and more students at the university level who are so used to having things done for them that they fail out of courses. When they do, there is always someone or something else to blame. Before auditions, I get asked what monologues they should pick, what day they should audition, even what parts they should audition for. It's as though the responsibility of...taking responsibility has been completely passed off to someone else like it's a hot potato. The writer of Proverbs says that the person who waits for the grain to be planted (instead of working through the summer like the ant) wakes up to find her house empty. He calls poverty a thief,[7] and I think it's because it gives the sluggard someone else to blame. It's true for sowing grain, it's true for succeeding in school, and it is absolutely true for anyone entering the acting industry. An actor who blames an agent for failing to bring a career to her door is like the man who blames the convenience store for not buying him the winning lottery ticket. The issue here is a combination of laziness and ignorance. Fortunately, both can be cured.

The Successful Actor

Starting out in a new field in a new market is daunting, and there can be many false hopes and dead ends along the way. It's true that a majority of an actor's life consists of rejection, but where people go wrong is how they handle that rejection. Most reactions to rejection can be put into two categories, and I suggest a third category as a viable alternative. When an actor sees the cast list for the next show, and her name stubbornly refuses to appear, she thinks it is either because she is inadequate, or the people behind the casting table are stupid (or nepotistic...or both). Both of these feelings form the causes for so many "former" actors littering the restaurants, car lots, and insurance offices throughout Los Angeles. They believe if they could just fix this one thing about themselves, or that if they could just party with or marry into the right crowd, all of their dreams would come true. After repeated failures, and without any tangible plan of action, most actors simply give up. The reality is they could be terrible actors, or the casting director only brings in people she knows, or neither of those reasons, but that isn't the point. Most performers (and I would say almost all of the people outside of the industry) have a fundamental misunderstanding of what an actor's job is and what it means for an actor to be "successful." It is (almost always) impossible for the actor to ever really know why she wasn't cast. Therefore, an actor needs to change her definition of failure and success.

It is easy for an actor to gauge how successful she is based on whether or not she is booking work. Even busy actors, however, will find long periods where the work just doesn't come. Does this make them unsuccessful? If being in plays or movies was the only evidence an actor had for success, then she is setting herself up for an emotional rollercoaster. She should, instead, amend her definition of success to better align with an actor's job, and an actor's job is to be seen. Granted, the most visible arena for an actor to be seen is on stage or in a film, but being seen can take many different forms. An actor can be seen at auditions and callbacks. Before that, an actor can be seen working in the industry (performing showcases, marketing herself, taking classes, honing her craft in workshops, teaching classes, producing her own work, or even working another job within the industry).

Think of the real estate agent. She needs to sell a house, but that isn't what she spends most of her time doing. She sets up an office in a prominent part of the town she wants to represent. She markets herself specifically to the people who live (or want to live) in that neighborhood. She teaches classes on buying a home. She connects with insurance agents and loan officers. She spends 40 to 60 hours each week doing all of these other things, so she can have six days that month where she is actually selling a home. If she looked at all the people she meets who don't want to buy or sell a home with her, she'd be a failure, and she'd probably quit (I would).

Now think of the actor who has just moved to a new city to start her career. The first priority is finding housing. Then, she has to pay for the housing (and transportation), so she finds a part time job. Many actors choose to work in the food service industry because of the fluid schedule, but right off the bat they find themselves now spending upwards of 30 to 40 hours each week actively not being seen. Food service jobs pay rather poorly (or sporadically if tips are involved). Bar tending pays more, but it also demands another skillset. Therefore, our young performer finds a second job to ease the cost of living off her back. Pretty soon, the actor has to juggle two work schedules to "fit in" an audition here and there. If I were my boss, and I saw myself working this type of business plan, I would fire myself immediately.

Preparation: The Art of Being Seen in a Positive Light

With all of this in mind, an actor's definition of success is directly related to how well she is representing herself in the marketplace. How often is she being seen, and by whom? Auditions are sometimes few and far between, which puts booking work even farther apart. This is why it is incredibly important that when an actor is seen, she is seen in a favorable light. If an actor sees a performance as the only place she will do her work, she is missing out on all the other opportunities she has to work her talents. Every rehearsal, every callback, every audition is a chance to perform a polished piece of art. That means an actor must be prepared. In addition to physical and vocal exercises, actors need to read. Read plays; then read the material the plays are based upon. Read biographies, histories, psychology, and behavioral economics. Read great literature, and read the trashy stuff everybody on the subway is reading. Then, when the audition comes, the actor has an arsenal of pop culture and historical references from which to pull. Most importantly, because of all of the literature she has consumed, she has become an interesting person, and interesting people get hired.

Above all (and I can't believe I'm even mentioning this) an actor must read the play/film she is working on. This isn't a singular, isolated read, either. The play should be read each day, with a pencil in hand. The script should be abused with notes, inspirations, and potential problems. An actor must know what every word in a scene means and how to use each word as a weapon within the scene. She has to come to the work with confidence where it is due, and intelligent questions where there is doubt. Gone are the days of "tryouts". An actor should never have to "try" to be a character in an audition. She has to come to her interview as though it were opening night of her five minute version of *Julius Caesar*. She has to come to a first rehearsal with the words of the play already living inside her. Her muscles must have already chewed the phrases of the play over and over again, so when direction comes, they (the words) aren't in the way.

Unfortunately, the prepared actor is the exception. This makes sense when one looks at the statistics. Only 10% of the workforce are booking jobs. The employed actor, then, is the exception, as well. One of the reasons is that many actors have no idea what is at stake. Money, reputation, or career advancement are strong incentives to give a strong effort. A play at a LORT A (top tier regional theatre in the League of Resident Theatres) pays close to one thousand dollars per week. Broadway contracts start at eighteen hundred per week.[8] Film and television scale even higher, and commercials are often even more lucrative. These scenarios are the brass ring, though, and the tunnel vision actors get often excludes all of the other work out there. They are willing to put in the work for the big projects, but the little ones get a lackluster effort. What some actors forget is that they are always auditioning. With the mindset that each project links to a future project, an actor will see the value of giving 100% to everything she does. The actor's reputation will earn her a spot on the audition list. Casting directors will notice an actor who consistently brings a thoughtful, interesting, and surprising performance, and they will often call that actor in for a role, even if she isn't exactly what the breakdown for the character asks for. Conversely, if an actor shows up for a first rehearsal, and they are unprepared, the likelihood of being hired back with that company lowers significantly (remember, the goal is to be one of the "same people" who always get cast). The stakes are even higher in an audition. At least the actor who is unprepared at the rehearsal will still get paid for the project. Casting directors are paid to remember actors, and this applies to both positive and negative experiences. An unprepared actor at an audition not only forfeits her chances at the role for which she is currently auditioning, she has reduced the chances of ever being invited back by the casting director. After that, the money, the reputation, and career advancement are impossible.

The Christian performer has even more at stake. She isn't working for the money, the reputation, or the career. She is working for the glory of God. The third commandment in forbids taking God's name in vain. When a Christian enters a secular workplace, she is quite literally taking God's name with her. The actor's work then becomes God's work, and to put in less than everything is to tear down the name of God. If, on the other hand, an actor is constantly striving to improve, prepared for intelligent and compelling work, and contributing a positive spiritual/emotional force within an ensemble, then God's name is glorified. Through the uplifting of His name, His message of redemption will spread. Through the quality of the Christian actor's work, ethics, and compassion, she will get to be part of God's plan (which is a far cry better than being a roadblock for it). The entertainment industry is a mission field, and the Christian actors who enter it must enter it as missionaries. It is unfriendly territory. There is much work to do to repair the centuries of damage done by Christians who have taken God's name lightly. With the right approach to the work, and the respect that approach engenders, the Christian actor will get work. Over time, she will earn a great reputation. With that reputation will come career advancement, which in turn will make her valuable. The more value the Christian actor has, the more the ears and hearts of the entertainment industry will open to what God is saying to His people.

DOING GOOD WORK – AUDITION CHECKLIST

Overview: Preparing for an audition is critical in developing a reputation for a good work ethic. How much should you prepare? How do you know when you're ready? The time frame for getting ready for an audition can be just 24 hours, so a checklist can really help you focus on what needs to get done. Using a checklist will allow you to get a good rest the night before an audition because you know you are fully prepared for the audition.

Instructions:

1. Read ALL of the material: this includes your scene(s), the crossed out parts of your scene(s), scenes for the other actors, the play/screenplay (if available), the stage directions, and the directions/time for the audition

2. Find at least three facts for each of the scene's given circumstances (who, what, where, and when).

3. Determine the best scene objective and obstacles.

4. Determine where in the scene "the switch" is. The switch is an opportunity for the character you are playing to change. This is usually a tactical change.

5. Come up with an intelligent, text based question for the auditor.

6. Memorize the scene. Most audition classes will not encourage this. I, however, find it extremely helpful.

7. Prepare for the trip to the audition: When do you have to leave? Do you need gas? Toll?

8. Print out three resumes and attach them to your headshot (three is the standard-make more or fewer if the audition instructions say so).

CHAPTER 6

The Line: Strangers in a Strange Land

"Art, like morality, consists in drawing the line somewhere."

\- G.K. Chesterton[1]

"I would do anything for love...but I won't do that."

\- Meatloaf[2]

The Question

Who we are is often wrapped up with what we do. We would all like to believe that good people do good things while bad people do bad things. This can lead to an interesting identity crisis for actors since they do so many different things. If we are constantly being cast as the villain, does that somehow make us evil? Admittedly, it is difficult for me to see an actor like Alan Rickman and not picture any number of the brilliantly evil men he has played, or an actor like Matthew McConaughey and not see someone who enjoys the company of pretty much anyone he pleases. In the cases of excellent actors, it is because they are so good at what they do that we are blinded to who they really are.

I teach acting to college students. We work on technique, discipline, and the business side of things; however, the question I get most often in class is about limits. It usually happens like this: a student will be cast in a show where he or she is asked to do something that puts him or her in an uncomfortable situation. The situation usually involves a question of morality. The student will ask, "Can I do such-and-such?" I have learned, however, that they aren't asking out loud what they really want to know. What they are actually asking is, "How far can I go and still be good with God?" That question has some pitfalls, making it difficult to answer. Asking it implies boundaries, and holiness knows no boundaries. When humans try to put a fence around God, the result is man-made religion, and the aim of this type of religion is suppression or behavior modification. Outside of fear, suppression is the last thing an actor needs when building a character. The other problem with boundaries is their effect on people. We relish exploring the borders in our lives. We sidle right up to the limits of permission, and we like to test, to push, and to investigate them. Think of Adam and Eve in the garden. They knew which tree to leave alone. They were told the consequences. Yet only three chapters into the book, there they are beneath its branches. But nothing happens. They reach out and touch the fruit. Again, nothing happens. They bring it to their lips...and nothing happens. The suspense is excruciating while they wait for the hammer to fall. I see the same picture repeating itself in my life every day. Is five miles over the speed limit too much? Is ten? How late can I leave and still arrive on time? On stage, the questions are even fuzzier. Can I hug this woman? Can I kiss her? What about more? To ask where our limits are belies a human desire to be freed from them.

That said, how far an actor can go without sacrificing his or her principles or identity is a valid question. The secular world deals with this same issue. For example, many famous actors will have something called a "nudity clause" in their contracts. The clause dictates the actor's specific unclothed body parts a director can use in a film. For all of the "openness" in Hollywood, there seem to be lines many actors won't cross. Where do these lines come from? The boundaries in question reflect an actor's worldview. To help answer our question of, "How far is too far?" we need to know where worldviews come from.

Worldviews

The two places actors (really all people, if we are going to be picky) go to form a worldview are a secular value system or a religious value system. Most of the secular world says our limits are self determined. All means are permissible if the ends are beneficial, and how beneficial the ends are is relative to the individual. Most secular actors will justify whatever they are asked to do in performance with the idea that the person on stage isn't them. They are simply playing a character, and the end result is either a good story or a paycheck (both, if you're lucky). Secularism can bend and shift to justify pretty much any choice and puts the actor in charge of their morality. A religious upbringing, on the other hand, hands out a list of acceptable and unacceptable behaviors. The list is determined largely by tradition, a sense of decorum, or a sacred text. This type of worldview can be stifling to an actor. It is difficult to perform any role when you have generations of reputation and tradition looming over your shoulder, whispering disapproval. Religion can also be used to justify one's self, and it provides a moral "out" for actors who have built up walls they do not wish to tear down. In the end, however, the secular world seems to offer the more attractive paradigm for a career in the theatre because a conservative worldview seems to limit the parts an actor can accept. Even though the world and our traditions each offer their own levels of safety and comfort, for an actor to discover his or her true limits, they need truth, and the truth is rarely safe and hardly ever comfortable.

In the book of John Jesus asks that we be sanctified by the truth, and He defines truth by saying God's word is truth.[3] Tradition and moral relativism each offer their own form of justification; however, God's truth offers something the previous two systems cannot: sanctification. I do not want to downplay the importance of justification, but being justified only goes so far. Strictly speaking, traditional or relative justification takes the offending party out of the position of guilt and places said party in a new position of relative righteousness. Sanctification goes deeper. The crux of sanctification includes justification (being declared legitimate by God), but then it goes one step further and sets apart the offender for God's purpose. It is this second step to sanctification that makes it such a frightening alternative to simply being "justified."

If sanctification is God's aim for the Christian, and God's truth is His primary tool for achieving it, it is extremely important to know what the Bible has to say regarding limits. Some care must be taken with the Bible because a person can look at something like the Ten Commandments and come to the conclusion that some magic list of do's and don'ts will keep him safe. Meanwhile, another person can find examples of God's people breaking laws left and right. This can lead him or her to determine that if Biblical characters have no obligation to moral responsibility, then neither does he or she. The casual reader

THE LINE: STRANGERS IN A STRANGE LAND

is left right back where he started, with religion or relativism. Then where is the line drawn? The Christian actor has to come to an understanding of what Jesus meant when He said, "Do not think that I came to abolish the Law or the Prophets; I did not come to abolish, but to fulfill. (NASB)"[4] How does a law fulfilled 2000 years ago affect the choices of an actor living today?

What Jesus did on the cross removed His followers from the burden of the law and introduced redemption through grace. Romans 8 says, "Therefore, there is now no condemnation for those who are in Christ Jesus, because through Christ Jesus the law of the Spirit who gives life has set you free from the law of sin and death." (NASB)[5] This puts Christian actors in a unique and sometimes confusing position. Is Paul saying the rules are off, and we can do whatever we want? Yes and no. Mostly no. We are free in Christ, but we still exist in a sinful world. Jesus told the woman at the well to, "Go, and sin no more." (NASB)[6] I take that as a commandment for all of us as well. While we are here (on earth), we must live as though we are dead to sin. I believe the reason Christian actors struggle with the issue of limits is because their definition of sin is broken.

Most of what society (and, admittedly, the church) sees as sin are physical actions, such as lying, stealing, and killing. However, using society's criteria for sin will only deliver society's justification, which we have already dismissed as ineffective. In Matthew,[7] Jesus raises the bar for what qualifies as sin to include the decisions or desires of one's heart. Using Jesus' standard, not only is murder considered a sin, but if our hearts hate our fellow humans, we're guilty of murder as well. Therefore, actors who are looking for a list of unacceptable actions are not looking far enough. Think of the physical actions people call sin as the fruit of sin, much like the physical manifestations of the fruit of the Spirit. In other words, sinful actions are apparent, but they were grown beneath the surface in the heart. We can take the example further and say physical actions do not constitute sin at all. In 1 Corinthians we learn, "All things are lawful for me, but not all things are profitable. All things are lawful for me, but I will not be mastered by anything."(NASB)[8] Paul adds a variation to this thought in the 10th chapter of the same letter: "All things are lawful, but not all things are profitable. All things are lawful, but not all things edify."(NASB)[9] There are two concepts here that give us an insight into what God considers sin. The first is mastery, and the second is edification. These two concepts, not society's acceptable mores, should be the barometer for deciding what is "profitable" and what is not.

Mastery

First, mastery is a dominant theme throughout the Bible. If I were bold, I would say it was the main theme. The question of salvation revolves around who has claim (lordship, mastery) over a person's life.[10] Romans 6 explains that we used to be slaves to sin, but have become slaves to obedience.[11] There isn't necessarily liberation in a Christian's life; it's more of a trade. We move from slave to bond servant. The main difference between the two is the slave is taken against their will, and the servant freely turns his life over to the master. A Christian performer should filter all of their actions through the lens of mastery. They should ask themselves, "Who is served by this action? Is it for my glory? Is it for my career? Or, is it for God and His kingdom?"

Another way to discern mastery is how it affects the actor's mind. Is the actor consumed with the action in question? Does it fill him with fear? Does he sacrifice for it? Or, is the actor consumed with God, and God's sacrifice?

Let us take a look at some specific scenarios to see how these questions work. "David" is married. He was cast in a play where he was directed to kiss his scene partner. From the outside, a kiss seems like no big deal. Stage kisses are pretty common, and the majority of actors have no problem with them. However, if I layer in a couple of "what if's" the picture gets a little muddy. What if David is attracted to his scene partner? What if his scene partner is only wearing a bikini? What if David's wife has asked him not to kiss this other woman? The trap here is to go back to society's definition of right and wrong. The mantra I hear most often is, "...as long as I'm not hurting anyone else." If David is attracted to his scene partner, it is more than likely he will be mastered in some way by this level of physical intimacy. The mastery is only compounded if the partner is wearing something revealing. Then again, what if he has no qualms about the kiss at all? What if his wife and friends are also fine with it? What if he isn't married, but he's dating someone else? Circumstances can shift, and moral decisions based on shaky ground can get us into trouble.

Meanwhile, "Melinda" has been cast in her first movie. She has grown up in a Christian home, and her parents are very conservative. In the movie, she has to use extremely provocative language, and there is one scene where she is to appear nude. Several factors come into play. Melinda might feel trepidation about her parents or church friends seeing her in this role. She might think swearing is wrong. She may also be concerned with how appearing nude in a movie will affect the rest of her career. She may also be cut from the project if she refuses to perform it as written.

Actors try to imagine the situations they will encounter to determine how they will react or what decisions they will make. As the two previous scenarios show us, "what if" scenarios (though fun for the actor) are inherently full of bottomless rabbit holes, and they cannot be depended on for a decision making foundation. A Christian actor needs something more than a "that depends" if he or she is going to feel safe on a set. The problem regarding an actor's personal, physical, and moral limitations has to come down to the answer of yet another, deeper question: *Am I actively pursuing God's kingdom?*[12] The timing of this question is vitally important. Asking this question only at life-altering moments is possible but not recommended. God will answer, but His answers often have unpredictable consequences in a human environment. For example, if Melinda is walking on to set the day she is to "bare all," and she hasn't thought to include God in her career, she is right to fear losing her job for refusing, or, on the other hand, alienating her parents if she goes through with it. At this point, if she asks God for guidance, Melinda will have to take whatever God's answer is and lay it on her producer or her parents with no warning whatsoever. Bridges may be burned, employment lost, or family wounds created. Unfortunately, it is only at crucial moments like this when most performers look heavenward. It is so easy to focus on getting work that the actor misses whether the work is worth getting in the first place. Then, after saying yes to a job, the actor is left to sort out whether God originally intended it for her, and fallout like Melinda's scenario is common. The question needs to come sooner. I have found that it is better to ask for directions before I leave the house, rather than in an unfamiliar (and sometimes unfriendly) neighborhood.

I tell my students that if they want to truly follow a Biblical method of acting, they need to include God in the entire process. This means that God is not merely a fountain of inspiration we tap as we make our first entrance on opening night, but He needs to be invited to our first rehearsal, our first auditions, even our first meetings with agents. Everyone involved in your career needs to be on the same page as you. This list includes: agents, managers, casting directors, producers, directors, stage managers, other actors, your spouse (yes), and God.

If any of these people are brought into the process late, conflicting messages and expectations are bound to blindside one or more of the parties involved. Therefore, actors must both ask themselves, "Am I pursuing God's kingdom?"[12] and their support system has to know that God's kingdom is the actor's ultimate goal. Then, when an actor meets an agent or manager, the agent and manager will know that the actor will be filtering all of their choices through a kingdom perspective. That way, when the audition comes around, the actor and his family will know God has led him or her to pursue this particular project. Then, when the job is offered, the actor can take it with confidence. Conversely, when the job isn't offered, the actor can know they were called simply to audition out of obedience. And finally, when it comes to shooting what some would call a questionable scene, the actor who has bathed his or her entire journey in prayer can relax into the familiar, consistent voice of God who has guided his or her steps from the beginning. Be warned, however, because God's thoughts are not our thoughts, His ways not our ways.[13] He may ask you to shoot the scene, or he may ask you to walk away. Either way, He leads, so hearing His voice and walking in the other direction is sin.[14]

It may look like I just said that it was okay to shoot a nude scene, and that may come as a shock to some people. In fact, I did not say it was okay to shoot a nude scene, but I did not say it was wrong to, either. Please remember the purpose of this chapter was not to lay out a list of acceptable behavior, or a roadmap to the human body complete with no-zones and go-zones. That is religion. Neither was the purpose to issue a cart blanche to follow whatever desires come around. No, the purpose of this chapter is to get the actor, who truly wants to perform in faith, to listen to the voice of God and obey. Acting in faith is exactly this process: the giving over of control of your life *and* your career. Some people may say, "My God would never (fill in the blank)." This phrase typically comes from people who are guilty of one of two things: 1) Having a narrow view of God's character (an infinite God doesn't bother with manmade limitations), or 2) Creating a God of their own who abides by their rules (a safe God who would never do anything unexpected). The Bible is full of examples of God doing things that would shock the pants off some of our Sunday-School-Flannel-Graph images of the Almighty. I like the way C.S. Lewis puts this in *The Silver Chair*, "Aslan is not a tame lion."[15] God is constantly doing the unexpected; He torments Saul with an evil spirit, He blesses tricksters and swindlers, He sends His son to die for mankind when mankind didn't want Him. So, when God says shoot a nude scene there may be some repercussions, but you had better shoot the scene. In these cases, remember Hosea. Here was a man who was asked to marry a prostitute.[16] I am sure his church friends had a thing or two to say about that. Remember Joseph (Mary's husband), who went ahead and married a woman who was already pregnant.[17] What did his parents think? By the same token, God may tell you to *not* audition for a role. Will another job come along? He may want you to stand up to your director. Will you burn a bridge? There's no way to tell for sure. More often than not, however, you will be put into a position to share the gospel you claim to be living out. At these times you will be glad to have allowed Jesus mastery over your career. It is much easier to share with colleagues the grace you have been given within the context of the world you work in.

The end of Matthew 6 tells Christians they cannot serve two masters,[18] so the actor has to choose who is in control of his or her career. Is it himself, or is it God? Can an actor be selfless if he doesn't allow God mastery over his career? Definitely, but there is no other reason to be selfless than his own desires to be nice or liked. If the actor is in charge, when difficult situations arise, he will eventually choose his success over someone else's. Inevitably, he will put his own needs first because there is a breaking point to a man's capacity for good. If, on the other hand, God has mastery over the actor's career, then the only thing the actor has to concern himself with is seeking God's kingdom. Then, when the difficult situations arise, he can lean on God who has an infinite capacity for doing good. Doing God's will, however, doesn't always mean the actor will get the role, or please the people around him. God is not welcome in all circles, and there will be times where the Christian performer, as the bearer of God's name, will also (because of His name) have to bear rejection and ridicule. For those times, Jesus offers reminds us that we are blessed when we are given the opportunity to suffer persecution and revulsion for Christ's sake.[19] Therefore, anyone entering any profession with the purpose of carrying the gospel forward should consider the fight laid out before them.

DEVOTIONAL

1. To aid you in interpreting God's plan for your career, the following verses should show how God wants you to approach troublesome situations involving morality:

   a. Hebrews 13:5-6

   b. 1 Corinthians 10:24-33 (pay special attention to verses 24, 28, 29,31 and 33)

   c. James 4:17

   d. Romans 14:1-23(pay special attention to verses 3, 14, 15, 20, and 21)

   e. 1 Corinthians 8:9-13 (verse 10 is the instruction, and the following verses are a great explanation of the instruction)

   f. 1 Corinthians 9:22-23

   g. Romans 6:1-2

   h. Matthew 10:16

   i. Romans 8:1-2

2. Give these verses a place of prominence in your life. Place them in highly visible places in your home. Come back to them often. As you change, God will speak to you in different ways. He promises to show Himself to anyone who seeks His face. The more you seek Him, the more you will find Him. The more you find Him, the more you'll come to trust Him.

3. Add to this list as God reveals His plans for you through His word. When you are faced with tough moral choices, you will have a treasure chest of God's wisdom to turn to.

CHAPTER 7

The Cost

" For which one of you, when he wants to build a tower, does not first sit down and calculate the cost to see if he has enough to complete it?"

– Jesus [1]

Acting is an expensive career, especially for a young performer fresh out of a training program. Like any small business, there is a certain amount of capital investment required. Headshots, classes, mailers, and subscriptions are all tools that are a continuing drain on the typical actor's bank account. Anyone entering the acting profession should take time to consider the cost much like Jesus' advice to those who wish to follow him. In addition to monetary costs, there are physical, lifestyle and spiritual costs to being an actor.

Physical Cost

In the same way professional athletes use their bodies to do their jobs, actors use their bodies to make their art. Therefore, body maintenance is of extreme importance. Brian O'Neil, author of the book *Acting as a Business*, once told me that one of the most important things for an actor to do for job security was to "embrace her type." The goal of maintenance, then, is to extend the length of a career without sacrificing your character type. This concept is often harder to grasp for my female students because the media is fairly brutal about its version of female beauty. Size, age, and the correct body proportions seem to be more strictly enforced on women. The reality is, however, quite different than the perception.

On the one hand, most of television and film is heavily influenced by advertisement. Therefore, a great deal of the men and women hired to sell to the strongest demographic (18-35 year-old men) are physically fit; the men have more muscles, the women have unattainable measurements, and everyone has flawless skin. The reason most young actors are so overwhelmed with body image issues is because they fall into the main demographic ad agencies target. In short, young actors are being bombarded with a lopsided view of the type of people who are working in the entertainment industry. On the other hand, there is work for every conceivable body type. In fact, the more unique the body type an actor has, the more likely she is to find work. There are many actors who leave the profession because they feel like they don't have the looks to get in the door, leaving it wide open for the actor with the unique body type who has had the discipline to persevere.

The ideal then, is to have a well adjusted attitude toward the body God gave you. The fact is you are fearfully and wonderfully made,[2] and God has plans for you, plans to prosper you not for calamity, to give you a future and a hope.³ There is a difference, though, between the body God created and a body abused by overindulgence and slothfulness. An actor adds years to her career by maintaining her individual body type through regular exercise, healthy eating, and reasonable stress levels, just as surely as ignoring these three things will cut a career short. Granted, there are short cuts to preserve a body type, like cosmetic surgery; however, someone who is convinced one particular physical feature is holding her back from the career she was meant to have has a fundamental misunderstanding of what an actor really does. There will always be another piece of the body that could use some help. That is simply part of living in a fallen world (you can blame Adam and Eve for not sticking to their diet instead of altering your body through surgery). Following is a list of physical activities intended to make the most out of what you were born with.

- *Yoga:* Yoga is a standard offering in most professional acting programs. It also carries a bit of a stigma as being a bit spacey, especially with more conservative sects of Christianity. I mention Yoga first for two reasons. The fact is, an actor needs to have control over his or her body, and Yoga is a terrific physical discipline. It increases flexibility and (muscle group) isolation, and it tones without bulking up the body. There can be some eastern spiritual elements intertwined, depending on the teacher. However, there are enough yoga studios now that it is relatively easy to find an instructor that is more "fitness oriented" than a spiritual guru. One of the main practices of yoga is meditation, but meditation in and of itself is not a bad thing. I have found it to be a great opportunity to meditate on a verse or a passage from the Bible. Simply use yoga as a time to listen to what God is saying to you.

- *Alexander Technique:* The Alexander Technique may not be familiar to many people outside the performance world, but again, it is fairly standard practice in actor training programs. Developed by Matthias Alexander around the turn of the 20th century, the technique aids the practitioner in efficient movement.[4] When the technique is practiced over time (and a good, private teacher is a must), the actor becomes more and more aware of needless tension present in everyday activities, such as sitting down, standing up, walking, and speaking. I appreciate the technique because it is a practical way to develop self awareness without self consciousness.

- *Dance or Sports:* These two activities are lumped together because they share benefits for the actor. Aside from team building or creative output, dance and sports keep the actor in shape, develop hand-eye coordination, and they are physical activities that constantly offer new and random challenges. Cardi-vascular health for an actor is often overlooked because actors feel like they have fairly active jobs. However, most of an actor's time (especially in film and television) is spent waiting, often sitting down. Having a team depending on you, or a class you've paid for is a great excuse to keep the heart healthy without changing your shape too drastically. Secondly, coordination for an actor allows her grace of movement. An athlete has a confidence of body that many actors would kill for. They are able to hold themselves still and move with purpose because they're body is ready to do whatever the situation calls for. Yoga and Alexander both work to enhance how the body moves, but they are both fairly predictable exercises. Sports and dance keep the performer on her toes, ready to respond in any direction based on the whim or actions of other people.

- *Gym Membership:* Going to the gym is the last on this list for three reasons. Working out is typically used to bulk up, which is a body altering activity, when body maintenance is the goal. There is nothing wrong with a toned body, but whatever the actor's body shape, he or she needs to make sure it aligns with the character type he or she wants to sell. Bulking up or slimming down for a potential role means the actor is fishing outside his or her character pond. Once a career track record has been established, then the actor can fluctuate her body shape to meet the needs of a role she ALREADY HAS. Dramatic shifts in body mass take their toll on a person's health, and an actor should always think about career longevity. Secondly, not many people know the healthy way to use the equipment at a gym, so the possibility of injury or inefficiency is high. Lastly, gym membership is fairly affordable. This may not seem like a drawback, but I have known too many people who pay the $50/month who simply don't go. It isn't a priority for them, and they don't miss the money enough to make it a priority.

Even in light of the three reasons listed above, gym membership offers some excellent benefits. A gym will often offer members access to Yoga or dance classes, which is a smart way to consolidate costs. Gyms are also a great way to meet other performers, especially in cities with a high concentration of artists like New York or Los Angeles. Finally, for actors who need to lose weight due to a lack of discipline in their eating habits or a sedentary lifestyle, the gym offers an affordable, designated location to "work" on their career. I find it extraordinarily helpful to "go to work". Whether that means finding a gym to work out in, or a coffee shop to write at, getting out of the house does two things for a person. The home has too many comforts and distractions to pull the professional away from his or her work. Secondly, there is a psychological benefit to dressing and leaving for work. Since much of the actor's life can be seen as sitting around waiting for the phone to ring, anything that gets the actor out of that mindset is a step in the right direction.

The other component of the actor's instrument is the voice. Regardless of whether you consider yourself a singer or not, your voice must be maintained with as much discipline as your body. There are exercises you can do to strengthen the voice, some of which are listed at the end of the chapter on work ethic. The voice is mentioned here, though, because there can be a significant cost associated with it.

The most obvious vocal expense is private study. Whether you are pursuing a musical theatre career or you are picking up a dialect, it is a good idea to have an outside ear you can trust, and they can end up costing quite a bit. One way around this is a barter for services. I know many actors who get their voice lessons in turn for editing performance videos for reels or even doing household chores. Enrolling in a voice lesson at a decent community college is an affordable option, as well. The importance of private study cannot be overestimated. The voice is a muscle, and singers are in competition with other performers who are just as talented, pretty, and friendly as they are, and the only edge they may have is how strong, flexible, and pleasant their voices are. If you were a body builder, you wouldn't think about entering a competition without a personal trainer. It's no different for the serious singer.

Material Cost

Small businesses need at least some capital in order to function. An actor should consider herself in the same light. Office supplies, marketing, and tools of the trade can all give the actor the infrastructure to be successful. Too many times actors will cut costs, but they won't know where to start. Often, a necessary expense will be reduced or removed in favor of what ends up being a want more than a need. Below is a list of tools an actor will find extremely helpful, a way to save money on them, and a description of how to use each tool for the greatest affect.

Office Supplies

- *Phone:* The most essential tool in an actor's office is the phone. Agents, stage managers, and casting directors all need instant access to the actor, and the phone is the way to make the actor available 24 hours per day. A phone must have these three functions: send/receive text messages, make/receive phone calls, and record voicemail. If an actor doesn't have a phone, or the phone service is unreliable, then she will lose work. Keep this in mind when choosing a company. Company A may be half the cost of Company B, but if Company A can't guarantee coverage outside of the city, then it may be worthless. I lived in a house that my cell wouldn't work in, but phones from other companies worked just fine. Phones with more features (like smart phones) can take on some of the functions of a computer and a calendar, enabling some consolidation of cost. Another way to be frugal is to combine plans. If an actor's family is supportive, asking to be included in the family phone plan can be a life-saver, but the actor should assume the cost of her part of the plan. I call this, "...having skin in the game." I would not recommend joining plans with roommates or significant others. There are too many variables with these types of relationships, and keeping monetary contracts to a minimum is usually a good idea.

- *Computer:* There are so many resources available to actors on the internet that some sort of a computer is a must. Audition information can be found on sites like nowcasting.com, backstage.com, and actorsequity.org. Many cities will also have a site listing professional and community theatre auditions, as well. Agents also welcome electronic submissions now more than hardcopies. Lastly, there are articles, podcasts, and publications easily accessible online that can go a long way to further an actor's education. Laptops, tablets, and even some of the "smarter" phones allow an actor to be mobile and connected. Being mobile is an important consideration since the actor's career will take her all over the world, and maintaining open communication channels is required for booking the next job.

- *Office Space:* When moving into a new city, a performer should seek out where the wi-fi hotspots are and determine which are most conducive to getting work done (remember the psychological benefit of leaving the house and going to work). It shouldn't be cost prohibitive, the distractions should be minimal, and there needs to be a friendly environment. For example, the coffee shop on the corner may have free internet access, but if everyone there knows who you are, your work time becomes social time. The things you should be doing online start losing priority. It is also a bit tacky to frequent a coffee shop or restaurant without purchasing something. The cost of lattes add up, so maybe a local library would serve as a better option. Prayerfully consider where and when you will work. It will allow you to know when you are on the clock, and when you can relax.

- *Calendar:* Electronic or hardcopy, a calendar serves two main purposes. Unlike most professions, an actor who is putting in the required work has multiple job interviews every week, sometimes while working on a project. Therefore, keeping track of auditions is critical. Secondly, a calendar can also be used as a budgeting tool. People say time is money, and at the beginning of an actor's career, she has a wealth of time to spend. Budgeting time is just like budgeting money. Dividing the day into segments for marketing, personal growth, creative projects, character research (if applicable), and rehearsal (if applicable), gives the actor the ability to know when she is on or off the clock.

- *Transportation:* Whether it is an automobile or public transportation, the key factor when choosing how to get around is reliability. Do the busses run every hour or every fifteen minutes? Does this particular car spend more time in the shop's garage than at home? The bicycle is by far the most reliable means of getting around, but a bicycle isn't very practical in a place like Los Angeles. An actor should research potential markets (cities) and then determine what sort of transportation the her target market requires.

- *Clothing:* Do not buy more clothes that you cannot wear for an audition, a rehearsal, or a performance. The same applies to haircuts. Audition clothing should align with your brand. If you want to play the sweet, girl next door, sunshine-in-her-hair ingénue, stay away from plunging necklines or combat boots. Auditions will come along where the slinky dress or the combat boots are necessary, but hold off buying out of character clothing until they do. All men should own a pair of hard-soled, black shoes, and women should have a comfortable pair of character shoes. Rehearsal clothes should be somewhat character-type specific, but their main function is mobility. I want my rehearsal clothes to get out of my way, both physically and mentally. I don't want to worry about ripping a hole in my pants, or worry about modesty issues when I have an odd pose or stretch to do. Women should have a floor-length skirt for period pieces, and men should have a suit coat. It is also a good idea to have rehearsal shoes similar to those being used in performance. A good costume shop will have a pair you can take out on loan. Performance clothing deals more with film than theatre. Like audition clothing, you should wait to purchase any clothing for a performance until you are offered the role. Don't throw away potential costumes. It may be a good idea for men to have a baseball outfit, or a pair of swim trunks in their closets. Military people should always keep their uniforms. The purpose of only purchasing clothing for your career is threefold. First, all of your clothing and hair expenses become tax deductible (ask your accountant how this works, and how much paid acting you have to do to qualify). Second, it will save you money. Simply asking yourself, "Do I need this for my business?" will put off those impulses to medicate yourself with a shopping trip. Lastly, and most importantly, it focuses you. When you begin considering everything you put on and into your body as a business expense, you begin to take your career quite seriously, even when no one else does.

Marketing

- Headshots: If there is an expense that is worth paying some money for, it has to be the headshot. Depending on the market, you can expect to pay anywhere from $150-$600+ for a good set of shots. Since the headshot is the first opportunity for agents and casting directors to see you, it has to be exactly how you want yourself to be represented. Shots for women range higher than men because a makeup artist is usually provided. Men should not discount the value of a good makeup artist, though, and they may want to consider hiring one as well. Money can be saved by bringing your own makeup and stylist, but whoever comes with you needs to know how to do makeup and hair for the camera. When comparing photographers look for the following: How many looks(outfit/hair/makeup changes) do you get? How long is your session? Will makeup be provided? Will digital touchup be included? Will you get all of the shots? Is there any kind of satisfaction guarantee? Look at the photographer's website or portfolio to see if he or she has any headshots that match the feel and type you are going for. Lastly, meet with them. Getting to know your headshot photographer is crucial for having a relaxed shoot. Also, when the photographer knows you, they can plan locations or music based on your personality.

- *Reel:* A reel is like a moving headshot. Like headshots, it is a good first impression tool. Unlike headshots, agents and casting directors also get to see you perform. As mentioned previously, the reel needs to showcase you and the people you have worked with. Gather and keep all of the footage from every film you have ever done. Comb through each film for usable material to put in the reel. Thankfully, there is software available at a reasonable price that puts the option in your hands of whether you would like to edit your own reel or not. Reels should be roughly 90 seconds in length. I advise doing a bit of research on established agency's websites, to see what sort of reels they use. Often, an agency will allow outsiders to watch some of the client's reels online. As your career progresses and competition gets tighter, hiring this job out to a company starts to make sense.

- *Website:* Whether it's your Facebook page or a fully dedicated site for your craft, protecting your online persona should be a top priority. Having a website is a great way to house all of your other marketing materials and to drive interested parties to the value of you. When should you buy a domain name or website? If you have a common name, snatch up a site as soon as possible. If you think your name or your brand is safe, you can hold off. Purchasing your domain name is relatively cheap and prevents it from being taken by anyone else. Social media like Twitter™, Facebook™, and Linkedin™ all link to your online identity. Everything you post/like/ignore is remembered by something, so be sure your posts reinforce your brand. Lastly, be aware of the hidden costs of websites. Make sure you are acting with integrity and paying for all of your pictures and music and giving credit to the other artists represented on your site.

The Spiritual Cost

In Timothy Keller's book *The Reason for God*, he talks about a woman in his congregation who came to the startling realization that her good deeds were getting in the way of the gospel. They were placing her in the imaginary position of a, "...taxpayer with 'rights'..." – The more work she put in, the more of a say she felt she had in her quality of life. However, after considering the great cost God paid for her salvation, she came to the conclusion that, "...if I am a sinner saved by sheer grace – then there's nothing He cannot ask of me."[5]

The process of hearing and obeying God's voice cannot be looked at as simply a means to better acting. Delving into the mind and will of God is a dangerous thing for those who are not willing to submit themselves to what God says. It is impossible to confine God to a single segment of your life. When you become more aware of God's leading on stage, you will also feel Him prodding you in your daily life as well. He will prompt you to do things that may seem counter intuitive, such as being late for an audition because a homeless person needed some help, not auditioning for a show because it would take you away from your family, or auditioning for a show even though it would take you away from your family. God may ask you to leave the acting profession all together. We have no idea what the specifics of following Christ will cost. Jesus says in Matthew 16:

" ... "If anyone wishes to come after Me, he must deny himself, and take up his cross and follow Me. For whoever wishes to save his life will lose it; but whoever loses his life for My sake will find it. For what will it profit a man if he gains the whole world and forfeits his soul? Or what will a man give in exchange for his soul? For the Son of Man is going to come in the glory of His Father with His angels, and will then repay every man according to his deeds." (NASB)[6]

The cost of inviting the Creator of the universe to guide your acting is the ownership of your soul. Every person has to ask themselves the same question Jesus asks us: *What will you give in exchange for your soul?* Our soul has to become as valuable to us as the blood spilled for it. If not, the lure of riches, fame, and power will be too great to resist, and our double mindedness will sabotage both worldly and eternal success. God promises that when we seek Him we will find Him.[7] The question, then, is what happens when we do?

The Christian actor will find it harder and harder to continue a career if she is hearing God's voice and ignoring it. This attitude shows a breakdown of belief in the actor's relationship with God. In the book of James, the writer is talking about the plans we make and our lack of regard for God's input. At the end of the section he says, "...to one who knows the right thing to do and does not do it, to him it is sin."(NASB)[8] We like to think of sin in black and white. Stealing is bad. Giving is good. Lying is bad. Going to church is good. What James is saying here is this: keeping silent when God wants you to speak is equally sinful as killing a person. I believe God wants Christian actors to be His voice in the entertainment industry. Maybe, like Jonah and Nineveh, the industry will hear God's words and repent. More likely, they will act like the Philippians and beat us out of town. Like Puddleglum in C.S. Lewis' *The Silver Chair*,[9] we have to accept the fact that God will often tell us what to do, but rarely will we hear what will happen when we do it. This "doing without knowledge" is how faith is fertilized.

It may seem unfair that people who do not believe in God seem to prosper by picking and choosing when to listen to His voice. It may seem that they are using inspiration for their own purposes and to great profit. However, a person who claims no knowledge or allegiance to God has no responsibility to do anything God says. Christians cannot expect people outside of the faith to act as though they are saved because people outside of the faith often don't feel like they need saving. They are unaware, though, that they are paying a price. People who reject God have exchanged their souls for the riches detailed in James 5. The riches he says have rotted away are money, power, or fame. If we are honest, these things do offer some level of satisfaction, but according to James, all of those things are doomed.[10]

Christians should respond to a text like James 5:1-3 with empathy and urgency. Empathy because we should all be able to remember when the things of this world obscured the reality of eternity for us.

Urgency because all of these people could very well die thinking this world is all there is. I have a hard time believing that at the end of all things, God's elect are going to be floating above the lake of fire rejoicing as each evil doer plunges into oblivion. God's super objective is not the punishment of the wicked. Jesus said He came to seek and to save the lost[11] regardless of the cost to Himself. Peter says, "He (the Lord)...is not willing that any should perish, but all should come to repentance."(NASB)[12] I believe we, as Christ's followers, should all be inspired to continue Jesus' search regardless of the cost to us as well.

There is no other way to study how the Bible applies to performance without addressing the foundation on which all of the principles of this book stand. In no way am I trying to say a performer outside the Christian faith won't be able to have peace, empathy or a desire to put someone else's needs before her own. I am more interested in the source of those virtues. Is it a temporal and conditional source, or is it a spiritual and eternally reliable source? All actors are free to choose what motivates and sustains them. The premise here is that Christian performers have a source unlike any other, and they would be foolish to hide it under a bushel in their professional lives.

All of the principles in this book come from an understanding of who we are in light of our relationship to God, or what one would call a "worldview." When one encounters God, one of two things happen: God is rejected or accepted. His holiness will either transform you into a humble believer, or it will be so frightening you will reject Him outright.

I will paraphrase Tim Keller and break it down this way: A person who comes face to face with the Holiness of God realizes they are far more corrupt and wicked than they ever dreamed. At the same time they know they are also more forgiven and loved than they ever thought possible. A person living in this reality will be patently humble, knowing the limits of their human condition, and innately confident, sure in their identity and purpose in Christ.[13] An actor of this sort will be fearless and meek, able to make bold choices while at the same time maintaining directability. Directors and producers will go out of their way to hire performers of this ilk, but there is a spiritual cost.

First, you will have opposition. It will come in many forms. You will encounter difficult directors and actors who will stab you in the back. You'll be ridiculed for your backwards, elitist, exclusionist beliefs. You'll have agonizing periods of unemployment. You'll have opportunities to act selfishly and hedonistically, and your family will be a battleground, as well. It is important for the actor who is following God's calling into the entertainment industry to realize her fight is not actually against any of these things, but there is a power in the world that strives to keep God's will from coming to fruition. Satan will use your colleagues, your doubts, your temptations, your circumstances, and your family to break you away from God's plan. Once the enemy has been named, it is far easier to deal compassionately with directors and actors, to forgive them, for they don't know who they're working for. You can undertake moments of doubt or temptation because you can recognize their common source. The fight can be tough, and there are sometimes casualties. However, your faith can grow if you remember that, "He who is in you is greater than he who is in the world." (NASB)[14] That is why James calls us to take joy in the struggles that come through our lives.

Much is said about the "free gift of salvation." And rightly so; God does not ask us to earn His grace. What He promises though, is once He is active in our lives we become new creatures.[15] As our will and God's will come closer and closer together, our old life passes away. It is not a matter of us changing ourselves to please God, but more about Him working the change in us to be more like Him. We lose our self-centered nature, and the desire to dominate our environment. The concept of losing one's identity is not a popular one in Western Culture, but it is the cost of following Christ. If the cost is too high, there are many other ways to unlock a good performance, as evidenced by the large numbers of amazing actors who aren't Christians; in the end, though, all they will be are great actors. A life with Christ promises, I would even say threatens, to make the Christian actor more.

Consider the cost before attempting to build this tower.

CHAPTER 8

The Actor's Toolbox

"Be diligent to present yourself approved to God as a workman who does not need to be ashamed, accurately handling the word of truth." [1]

– Paul's second letter to Timothy

In the chapter on Inspiration I mentioned a method of Bible study using the tools I was given for studying Shakespeare. I felt it was a good idea to lay out the method and the tools in their own separate chapter since so many of the concepts in this book really hang on a uniquely theatrical understanding of God's word. My Shakespeare professor in graduate school, Jim Winker, brought to life an author and characters I had long thought inaccessible or irrelevant. In turn, the thorough textual analysis required for class made me realize I had the same unspoken prejudices regarding the Bible. Like most young Christians, I respected God's word. However, I didn't give it the place in my life it deserved until the people, places, and events it talks about came to life in the same way the people, places, and events of Shakespeare's world come to life: through careful and intentional study.

The Method: Super Objective and Given Circumstances

One of the arguments atheists have against religions is the incomprehensible barbarism apparent in many of the holy texts on behalf of the ruling deity and the deity's followers. Christopher Hitchens talks of the Bible's perceived tolerance for slavery, genocide, and "indiscriminate massacre."[2] I have to admit there were parts of the Bible that struck me in much the same way. It is difficult to look at Jacob and Isaac and not see Jacob's deception of his father as wicked and cruel.[3] I also couldn't get my mind around a God who would send an evil spirit to torment the man He chose to be king.[4] Without a full trust in Scripture, my desire to read it grew less and less. Eventually, parts of the Bible that were hard to understand or troubling were either glossed over or ignored the few times I would sit down for study. That is, until I began looking for dramatic clues like given circumstances and objectives.

Upon discovering a character's given circumstances, which tell us the foundation of a character, we uncover something called the super objective. An objective is what a character wants to accomplish in any given scene. The super objective is what he is fighting for over the entire arc of the play. Each scene may show us a different, sometimes shocking aspect of the character. Taken out of context, an "evil" character can seem benevolent, or a "good" one downright despicable. In light of the super objective, however, these actions all make sense as the character makes his way to his desired end.

When I learned about the concept of the super objective, I applied it to the Bible. Concentrating less on morals, I searched instead for given circumstances. What were the *facts* about these characters. I can see how Joseph was left for dead by his brothers when I look at Jacob's (Joseph's father) habitual pattern of favoritism.[5] The story of Noah's ark changes from a story about animals when I realize at the end of it that everyone else on the planet is dead. I began looking at the Bible not as a series of plot points, but as a cohesive, linear, love story with a protagonist and an antagonist. In true dramatic form, these two players have diametrically opposed super objectives, and the stakes are high. I mention the stakes because it helps me see why God seems to stop at nothing in His quest to redeem humanity. Now, when I hear of God tormenting King Saul with an evil spirit it isn't cruel, considering He could have killed him for disobeying. Looking at the super objective, I see throughout the book of 1 Samuel God *sparing* the life of Saul over and over again in hopes the king will turn back to the One who put him on the throne.

Knowing some of God's given circumstances (His omnipotence, omnipresence, omniscience, and the love He has for us), knowing His enemy (Satan and his agents. According to James, the proud also fall into this category[6]), and knowing what is at stake (the eternal fate of the universe), transformed my perception of the Bible into something I could easily relate to as an actor. The story of the Bible has the drama of opera, the spectacle of musical theatre, the profound wisdom of a great play, and the personal intimacy of an indie black-box show. I have had a belief in God all my life, but this relatability was key to my interest in what He had to say to me. If only I could understand it.

The Text

Both the Bible's and Shakespeare's language are difficult for a number of reasons. There are the problems of antiquated speech, double and triple meanings for words, and imagery that isn't readily accessible to a 21st century audience. This should not be surprising since both Shakespeare and King James were contemporaries, and King James was instrumental in passing on the most widely distributed English "version" of the Bible.

At the University of San Diego, I learned a method of breaking down text that allowed me to find the sense of the line and the breadth of the thought. As I was going through this course, I was also reading one of Paul's letters. I noticed a similarity in construction between Shakespeare's and Paul's writing that made me think I could use the same principles I was learning in literature class on the Bible.

The first step to understanding Shakespeare and the Bible is knowing specifically what the words mean. It sounds simple, but there is a vast difference between a general idea of what a line says, and knowing *specifically* what the line means. General productions of a Shakespeare play can be deadly just as a general idea of a Bible verse can lead us astray. For Shakespeare, there are several tools at our disposal to help define words.

The Tools: Shakespeare

The easiest option for defining Shakespeare's words is to buy several editions of the plays. These will have different styles of editor's notes based on the company, such as the Oxford, Arden, Cambridge, or Penguin editions. I have found the Oxford and Cambridge editions' notes are focused on the actor, and the Arden's more scholarly notes are better suited for the director. The Penguin is the cheapest edition on the list, but they do have some decent definitions and pictures. The benefit to having a well-edited version of the play is that the notes are on the same page as the text, and it doesn't slow the reader down. Gather multiple versions of the play because no edition defines everything. When the notes fall short, the actor must consult outside sources for help.

The second, and more comprehensive tier of reference materials, are the Shakespeare Lexicons published by Dover Publications, and the Oxford English Dictionary (OED) now available online. The lexicons are a two volume set, and I've seen them for sale online for less than $5.00 each. They list every word Shakespeare wrote, and they define how the word is used in each case. Context is immeasurably important when defining words, and the lexicons provide quotes from the plays to show the word's usage. The OED is also a huge help, but it carries with it a huge price tag. Though it may be cost-prohibitive to own a copy, you can access it through most libraries' computer systems. The OED provides multiple definitions as well as something called the etymology of words. Etymology details the origin of words, along with the approximate year it was first used. Shakespeare's time was a ripe one for crafting new words and the tweaking of old ones. I like the OED because it helps to know how many meanings of a word were around when Shakespeare was writing. Chances are, he meant at least two of the existing definitions, and if he didn't, at least it gives the actor something to play with.

Lastly, listen to the words of the play through whatever means you can. There are hoards and hoards of recordings of Shakespeare's work, and you can find them in all types of media. Watch the movies; listen to CD's; go to Youtube and search for Shakespeare; you may even want to go crazy and watch a play at a theatre. This should be the last layer of your research since there are so many bad performances of the cannon. It is still helpful to have this layer, though, since the plays were written to be spoken out loud.

The more you devote yourself to the words, the more you will find you are looking up things you thought you already knew. I tell my students to look up everything because even a word like "oh" can have double or triple meanings (and it does).

The Tools: The Bible

Bible study will follow the same pattern of research as play analysis. Since the Bible probably wasn't written in your native language, I recommend using several versions of the Scriptures to get a wide variety of interpretations. Some editions may be too "heady," some may sound like slang, and some will feel like home. There is an overwhelming amount of versions available, but thankfully, most of them can be found online. I use a website called biblegateway.com, and it has many of the mainstream versions of the Bible as well as a decent cross reference program. Authenticity should be a major concern, so take a look at how each version of the Bible you choose was composed.

Some Bibles are interpretations, and some are translations. Interpretations are taken from a number of different sources. Most of them are compiled using existing translations, and the editors have modified the text to suit a particular demographic or purpose. The purpose behind an interpretation is to make the language and concepts easier to grasp. There are certain problems inherent with interpretation. They are, at best, second hand accounts. There is a risk of losing material, especially if the reader does not happen to fit exactly into the edition's target demographic. On the other hand, the best part about them is they can offer a fresh way of looking at a passage that has grown too familiar to hold the same meaning it once had.

Translations take the original source material, and the editors try to capture what the author wrote in another existing language. There are a few literal translations available, but they are a difficult read due to verb tense and syntax. I like them because the subtle differences individual words have in various interpretations can be cleared up by seeing how the phrase was originally constructed. Most other translations involve a bit of interpretation as well, but the source is only one step away (instead of two like an interpretation). I find translations to be more reliable than interpretations because the editor's focus is on the author's intent rather than the audience's comprehension. Whichever versions you choose, they should all have notes on the text. I use a MacArthur or a Scofield reference Bible, and the notes on locations and contemporary customs are invaluable. There are also commentaries available for each testament and individual books, but many times they won't include the full Biblical text. Some books are more scholarly than others, so it is a good idea to peruse a Bible's notes before you purchase it.

Just like Shakespeare, the various editors' notes of the Bible can only go so far in helping us to decipher words and usage, so we must find outside tools to supplement our study. The OED is a great help once again. Use it in the same manner described in the sections above for etymology and meaning. In addition, most Bibles in stores have some form of concordance located at the end of the book. In my opinion, the better concordance makes a better Bible. Concordances act in the same way the Lexicons do for Shakespeare. They take a word, and they show where it's used other places in Scripture. The best concordances also show *how* the word is used as well. Strong's exhaustive concordance is even more comprehensive, and it is available online. Biblestudytools.com has a very easy to use tool system, and eliyah.com has a more advanced search feature as well as Hebrew and Greek lexicons, so you can see the original word as well. Hebrew and Greek often use compound words that give us a better picture than the English equivalent. In fact, the key to using these tools is to not take for granted our knowledge of English. The particular translation you use can give you a false sense of getting the whole picture. Be diligent, and do not settle for a "general" idea of what the Scriptures are saying.

Finally, you should be listening to the Bible. Just like a play, the Bible was meant to be memorized, read aloud, and quoted in the public square. As actors, the material, the scope of the lines, the engaging and difficult dialogue are all reasons we should be hungry to get these words in our mouths. The public reading of scripture has taken a back seat in many mainstream churches. Many sermons will take only a few verses, and rather than ask the congregation to pick up their Bibles, the one or two verses will be projected on to the screen. I have sat through many services where people do not touch their Bibles at all. We need to hear the Word of God. When you have your private study, read aloud. At your church, approach your pastor, and volunteer to read in the service, or in Sunday school, or in your small group. Find a nursing home and read to people who no longer can on their own. I won't write the benefits of reading aloud here because the more you serve in this way, the less the benefits to you matter.

Bible Study Example

How do these tools work in Bible study? Let us examine a familiar Bible story and see if given circumstances and objectives can help us relate to the characters better. Growing up in a Christian home, I heard the story of "doubting Thomas" many times. The story, found in John 20, shows Thomas talking with his friends about the resurrected Jesus.

> "But Thomas, one of the twelve, called Didymus, was not with them when Jesus came. So the other disciples were saying to him, "We have seen the Lord!" But he said to them, "Unless I see in His hands the imprint of the nails, and put my finger into the place of the nails, and put my hand into His side, I will not believe."

Thomas doesn't believe Jesus appeared to the disciples, and a few verses later he comes face to face with Christ.

> "After eight days His disciples were again inside, and Thomas with them. Jesus came, the doors having been shut, and stood in their midst and said, "Peace be with you." Then He said to Thomas, "Reach here with your finger, and see My hands; and reach here your hand and put it into My side; and do not be unbelieving, but believing."

Thomas believes Jesus is who He says He is, and we are left with Christ's admonishment: "Because you have seen Me, have you believed? Blessed are they who did not see, and yet believed." [7]

Most Sunday school lessons end there with a, "That's why we should always believe Jesus," from the teacher. Frankly, that always left me unsatisfied. Was there any more to Thomas that might help me understand how God interacts with His people? The given circumstances will guide us to answer that question.

What do we know of Thomas:

- One of the twelve disciples called specifically by Jesus
  - In Matthew 10 he is listed 7th with no description
  - In Mark 8 and Luke 6 he is listed 8th with no description

- Given a host of special gifts in Matthew 10, among them are:
  - Authority over unclean spirits
  - Healing of every kind of disease and sickness, including death

- Was present for most of Christ's ministry and witnessed miracles

- His alternate name in John 20 was Didymus, which means "twin"

- He goes fishing with the disciples the day after seeing and believing in the resurrected Christ
  - He is listed 2nd

- In John 11:16, he was willing to die for Jesus before Jesus died for him

What do we know of Jesus (this isn't an exhaustive list):

- He told His disciples He would die and come back three days later

- He died and came back three days later
  - Hardly anyone he encountered believed it was him
  - He bore the wounds of His execution
  - He could be touched, seen, and heard

- He performed many miracles

- He was only staying on the earth for a little over a month after His resurrection

- – Responsibility for delivering the gospel was being transferred to the disciples

• In Matthew 9:4 it says He knew the hearts of men

Now that we know this information about Thomas, we can put ourselves into his shoes. The first time we see Thomas in action is right after the news of Lazarus' illness has reached the disciples in John 11. They don't want Jesus to go because He's a wanted man there. Ironically, Thomas shows no doubt here and offers to accompany Jesus in the face of great danger. Up until this point, Thomas has seen nothing but Jesus come through on His promises, and Thomas is fearless.[8] The next time this disciple speaks is in John 14:4-6, Jesus answers with, "I am the way, the truth, and the life; no one comes to the Father but through Me." Whenever anyone asks Jesus a question, He answers their heart.[9] The Pharisees were a great example of this. They would try to trap Jesus in a sticky bit of the law, and instead of falling into their schemes, Jesus will ask another question or pose a story. Thomas needed to hear that Jesus was the way, the truth, and the life, and Jesus knew it.

Fast forward then to when the only way to salvation was killed on a cross. Three days later, Thomas hasn't seen his master come back. To Thomas, the last three years of his life were now a waste. He loved Jesus, as evidenced by his willingness to die with Him. Then, Thomas' friends claim to have seen the resurrected Jesus. Given his nickname, Thomas might have thought the person his friends saw could very well have been a twin. However, if I were to step into Thomas' place, I get a different, more human, picture. I am imagine thinking:

I was with Jesus for three years. I saw Him perform miraculous signs. We spent intimate moments together, eating, praying, talking about the shape and future of the world, and my part in it. I believed

He was the answer to all of my problems. I was willing to follow Jesus into death, and who does He appear to? Some women, and that screw-up, Peter.

I can relate to Thomas now. I can remember a time when I had an expectation of God He didn't meet. Thomas' doubt comes from a place of grief, but there is also likely an element of hurt and shame. Hurt, because I would have felt like an outsider around all of these men I called friends. Jesus picked them over me. I can almost hear him say, "Why not me first?" while he's asking to see the wounds. I would also feel shame, because I would know in my heart that I would be listed 7th in the order of the disciples. Jesus knows my heart. He knows what I've said about Him in private. Immediately after appearing in the room, He looks directly at me and says, "...do not be unbelieving, but believing."[7] He knows there would be nothing to distinguish me from any of the others. Lastly, He knew how important those last few words would be to me, and to the rest of humanity, " Blessed are they who did not see, and yet believed."[7]

Does this story teach a moral? Maybe, but what I get out of it is a glimpse into the character of God. I don't see the word doubt in this small story nearly as much as I see the word "believe." Believe is used many times in the New Testament. It's Strong's number is 4100. It talks about being persuaded, or giving credit to something. I latched on to the word credit because I know where it comes from. A bank will not loan me money until I have developed a track record of paying it back. Jesus is asking Thomas to look back on their relationship and extend the credit of belief, and He is putting forward His resurrected body as proof or collateral. I am then forced to look back at my own life to see the many places Jesus has built up His credit with me. When I do, I realize my faith is not blind. Instead, it is grounded in the consistent providence of an invisible, yet palpably involved God.

I also see Jesus knowing the heart of His follower. I see Him give His disciple exactly what he asks for, to touch the wounds himself. I see God pursuing his followers, and adapting to meet each of their needs. I see how He spoke to me through my acting, and turned me from unbelief to belief. I also see the power of belief after an encounter with God. When the men all go out fishing the next morning...

Thomas is listed 2nd.[10]

Appendix

EMPATHY EXERCISE 1

You Be Me

Props: None

Cast: Medium to large ensemble and a director

Time duration: Long (approximately 15 minutes per pair)

Overview: Use this exercise as a way to both introduce students to each other and to introduce the concepts of observation, improvisation, given circumstances, and permission.

Instructions:

- Break the group up into pairs

- Give the pairs 3 minutes each to interview each other

- Tell the actors to pay special attention to their partner's vocal patterns, body language and demeanor.

- After the interview, the actors will introduce themselves to the class as their partner. For example: Erik interviews Jenifer. When Erik introduces himself to the class, he introduces himself as Jenifer; he uses Jenifer's facts, vocal patterns, body language, and demeanor.

- The director will then open up the introductions to questions for the rest of the ensemble. The deeper the questions the better; however, the director should allow the ensemble to drive the interview without too much interference. Example: The ensemble asks Erik (as though he is Jenifer) about the hardest part about being a girl, or about her first kiss, etc.. It is up to Erik to fill out the rest of Jenifer's story using only the details he gathered from the interview and his imagination.

EMPATHY EXERCISE 2

The Facts of Life

Props: Writing surface (paper if an individual exercise or whiteboard if an ensemble exercise)

Cast: Individual to large ensemble (use a director if there are more than a pair)

Time duration: Medium (approximately 10 minutes for individual, ensembles can take up to 30 minutes)

Overview: Use this exercise to separate fact from fiction while building a character. The exercise also sheds light on understanding another person's given circumstances, allowing empathy for difficult personalities.

Instructions:

- Separate your writing surface into four quadrants and label them #1-4. Give yourself room to write.

- Have the individual or the ensemble pick a celebrity to describe.

- Write down every single thing the ensemble says in the first quadrant. Be ready to write small. The more descriptions, the better. There are no wrong answers.

- Pick one actor from the ensemble to describe his mother.

- Write down everything the actor says in quadrant #2. If there are other people present who know the mother in question, allow them to contribute as well.

- Pick another actor from the ensemble to describe a person with whom they have had a conflict. It's not politically correct, but ask the ensemble if anyone has an enemy (I usually say "nemesis". It tends to lighten the mood.) The stronger the dislike, the more effective the exercise is.

• Write down everything the actor says in quadrant #3. If there are other people present who know the nemesis in question, allow them to contribute as well. It will be tempting to defend the nemesis (especially if you are doing the exercise on your own), but it is better to wait until the end of the exercise. Hopefully, the next few steps will go a long way in developing understanding for him.

• Pick a favorite movie character to describe.

• Write down everything the ensemble says in quadrant #4.

• Go back through each of the quadrants and separate fact from fiction. Find out which qualities are indisputable (e.g. divorced, 6'1", dyed hair, unemployed), and which are judgments or opinions (e.g. flirty, smart, vain, pretty).

• Use the facts to find the connections to the judgments.

• Fill in as many more facts about the people in each quadrant.

Johnjacobjingleheimerschmidt

(Adapted from an exercise created by Lucas Caleb Rooney)

Props: None

Cast: Individual to large ensemble

Time duration: Variable (Anywhere from a few seconds to an entire class period. The director can return to this exercise at any time for any length of time)

Overview: Develop actors' ability to collaborate truthfully and give over their individual ideas to a central idea. Saying "No" is a large part of this exercise, and it should be encouraged. The ensemble will learn to trust each other to tell each other's story.

Instructions:

- Have the ensemble sit in a circle (or equally comfortable arrangement: lying down, backs to each other, etc.)

- One member of the ensemble will say a name. Do not use the names of "real," identifiable people. The name can be in any configuration (e.g. Tom, Murphy, Mrs. Bedelstein, Little Bobby, Angus the Fire-Eater, etc.).

- After the name is said, the game opens up to the entire ensemble. They need to build onto the name only using facts (not judgments). Each fact will further build the newly created character's world. If a fact is considered true by the rest of the ensemble, play continues. If, at any time, a fact is mentioned, and even one of the ensemble considers it "out of character," that ensemble member will say, "No." When a "no" is said, the character in progress dies, and someone else within the group begins a new character by saying a name. A good way to determine whether or not a fact will kill a character is by considering where the desire to contribute that fact comes from. Does it come from a desire to be funny? Or, does it come from the world that is being created? For example, it might be out of character to say Herb Lawson slays dragons if the ensemble has built a world where dragons do not exist, but it may be perfectly legitimate for Ragnar of the Mountain People to do so. The goal is to be truthful. There should be no pressure on the ensemble to be interesting (interesting will automatically happen).

- The pacing of the game should be maintained by the director. If it gets too fast, that usually means there are competing personalities within the ensemble vying for control. The director needs to encourage overly competitive actors to let go of control. If the pacing is too slow, ensemble members are probably afraid of either saying "No," or they are afraid their ideas will be rejected.

- This exercise can be done individually. Simply write the facts on paper or a word processor. It is more difficult to kill these characters, but it is important to be just as strict with only using true facts. The characters created can then have objectives and obstacles put in their way for a good writing exercise.

Grab Bag Scenes

Props: Four containers for slips of paper (hats, boxes, etc.), pencils, small slips of paper (about 14 per person), whatever is in the playing space can be used within the scenes

Cast: Medium to large ensemble and a director

Time duration: Medium (approximately 5 minutes for setup and 10+ minutes to play - each scene should take less than 2 minutes)

Overview: Actors will use facts to build a scene. The exercise is designed to be short in that it shows the limitations of only playing given circumstances.

Instructions:

- Set out the four containers and label them: Who, What, Where, and When

- Hand out the slips of paper to the entire ensemble. Have them write five facts for each of the following categories: What, Where, and Why. Have them write out ten facts for "Who".

- Place the slips into the matching containers.

- A pair of actors will each take a slip from the "who" container.

- The pair will share slips from the "What, Where, and When" containers.

- The pair then acts out the scene using only the facts they are given. The director needs to "Buzz" in when the actors use facts not informed by the slips of paper. This is a little tricky, but a good rule of thumb is to consider this: If fact A is true, then what else has to be true? For example: The "Where" is in Antarctica. If that is true, then there is also snow, there are penguins, there is extreme weather. All of those things are "playable" in the scene. Having a lion come in would be far less likely, and the director should redirect the scene.

- The scene should strive to get to two minutes. It will be difficult because most of the time there will be no conflict.

EMPATHY EXERCISE 5

Contentless Scenes

Props: The ensemble can use whatever props they bring in or are already present within the playing space. The director must supply contentless scenes.

Cast: Pairs

Time duration: Medium (approximately 30 minutes to a couple of days for prep, 2 minutes for execution)

Overview: The acting pair must collaborate to create facts and conflict within a scene where no facts are given. Then, those facts must be clearly communicated within a scene. Giving the acting pairs more time (outside class) is best for this exercise.

Instructions:

- Split the ensemble into pairs.

- Distribute the scenes to the pairs.

- Have the pairs collaborate to determine their relationship, action, location, and moment before/after.

- Have the pairs collaborate to determine opposing objectives.

- Give the pairs rehearsal time.

- The pairs will give their list of given circumstances and objectives to the director. Then they will perform their scene for the rest of the ensemble.

- The ensemble will then have to guess what each of the given circumstances and objectives are based on the performance. If the guesses are close, then the next pair will perform. However, if one (or more) of the given circumstances or objectives is incorrect, have the pair leave the playing space and come up with a way to play the scene in order to better communicate that particular aspect of the scene.

Script Scoring

Props: A script, a highlighter, and a pencil

Cast: Single person or pairs

Time duration: Short (approximately 10-15 minutes per 3 minute scene)

Overview: Highlighting a script is a practical way to take the focus off of yourself and put it on your scene partner. The "Inspiration" chapter has an in-depth reasoning behind the scoring. Throughout this book, there will be things to add to this exercise. For example, from the "Empathy" chapter, you can write your objectives directly in your script, so you can see them when you work. Writing out possible tactics would also be a good idea since your tactics will be focused on your scene partner. Scoring your script in this way also makes it easier for someone to run lines with you. Suddenly, all of their lines are highlighted, and if you need any extra help remembering your lines, you can ask your helper to tell you what you have indicated as your trigger.

Instructions:

- Break your script into French scenes. A French scene begins when any character enters; it ends when any character exits.

- Choose one scene to score. A two-person scene is ideal.

- Highlight all of your cue lines (the lines immediately before your own).

- With your pencil, put a box around all the words and actions you feel your character responds to. These are called "triggers."

- Use your pencil to underline your partner's triggers.

APPENDIX

- Use Isabelle in the following scene as an example:

HIGHLIGHTING KEY

Cue Line | **Trigger** | **Partner's Trigger**

A young man (Hector) enters with a young woman (Isabelle)

ISABELLE

Oh Hector, why can't you take me away from all of this, so our love can blossom like a wild cactus?

HECTOR

You know I would do anything to be with you, my darlingest. But mother is oh so very lonely.

ISABELLE

You are a grown man, now. Don't you think it's about time you asked your mother for that ring of hers?

HECTOR

I do. And I will. But I shouldn't. So I can't.

ISABELLE

I'm sixteen years old, Hector, and my womb is withering!

167

HECTOR

Now Isabelle...

ISABELLE

It withers, I can hear it! If you won't sweep me off my feet, perhaps there are other brooms in the closet.

Hector pulls Isabelle in close.

HECTOR

Isabelle, I had better be the only broom in your closet.

ISABELLE

Well, maybe you should come out of that closet of yours and show me what kind of man you really are.

He turns away in agony.

HECTOR

I can't, love-duckling. Mother sent me out to find a chef for tonight. If I'm not home in an hour, she'll have my head.

ISABELLE

(Furious)

Hector, if you can't love me like your mother, I'll find a man who can!

She exits, weeping as she goes.

HECTOR

But Isabelle! Isabelle?!

INSPIRATION EXERCISE 1

Are You Listening?

Props: None

Cast: Small to large group (5+ people)

Time duration: Short (depending on the group size)

Overview: Part of readying your body and your mind to be lead by inspiration is to get rid of the one thing rehearsal is so good at building: a plan. So often actors execute a production like they were checking off items on a to-do list. Actors trained in this way will get lost if anything goes wrong. Granted, there needs to be an agreement among the actors, the director, and stage management about what is and is not acceptable in performance. However, planning out a reaction is the last thing you want to do. Instead, if you plan on anything, plan out what you would like to do to your castmates, tactically, throughout the show. That way, they can depend on the intention of what is coming at them, but the performance isn't flat because you aren't prepping for the next emotion you get to play. This exercise is designed to practice spontaneity within a brief and repetitive script.

Instructions:

- Group forms a circle.

- 1 participant leaves the room (or covers their ears). The participant should take time to pray and clear his head of any noise.

- The group is given one question from the leader, such as, "Where were you yesterday?"

- Each member of the group takes time to choose their own tactic/ intention for the line (i.e. to frighten, to anger, to flatter, to entice).

- The participant outside moves to the center of the circle.

- Each group member takes turns asking the actor in the center the question. The actor on the outside of the circle should get the actor inside of the circle's attention. This can be done with a simple, "Hey! (Question)." The point being, the "asker" cannot begin their question until they have eye contact with the "answerer".

- The answerer then responds to the question based on the words, the body language, the tone, and the perceived intent of the "asker". Each time the actor in the circle responds, he should attempt to repeat the same words he used for the first question. If an actor is forced to use a different phrasing, consider what it was about the stimuli that caused him to do so.

- For an added challenge, the actors on the outside of the circle ask their questions in a random order. Each member must listen for an opening and declare their intent to speak with only an inhalation of air.

INSPIRATION EXERCISE 2

Who's Telling the Story?

Props: Use whatever is in the room.

Cast: Small to Medium

Time duration: Long (approximately 30-40 minutes total)

Overview: Inspiration doesn't always come to us directly as God's voice. Honestly, it rarely does. Often, he uses the people and circumstances around us to get us to act (both in daily life and on stage). Listening and responding is another way of reacting to inspiration. This exercise is separated into two parts, and each requires letting go of your own agenda and adding to someone else's ideas for the good of a story.

Instructions:

- Split the group in half, and get each half to sit in a separate circle, preferably with a good distance between groups. If there are more than 11, split into three groups. If there are more than 15, split into four.

- Each member of the group will take turns creating and adding to a story for 30 seconds per person. The rules of improv apply. If someone says, "Once upon a time there was a boy," the next person can't invalidate it with, "But the story's not about him." The idea is to build off of each other's story by listening and giving.

- Depending on the size of the group, the cycle should complete itself multiple times. A good rule of thumb is 6-8 minutes total time.

- After the story is complete, each group appoints a story teller. The story teller is obligated to tell the story as authentically as possible.

- While the story teller is narrating, the opposite group will act it out. They should not be silent actors, and the narrator should give them time to speak and add to the story in unexpected ways. Both the narrator and the actors need to be listening for opportunities to make each other look good.

- The second group then takes over telling the story while the first group acts it out.

Breathing and Feeling

Props: A safe environment, a chair, and freedom from interruptions

Overview: Physical action and emotion are linked through breath. After studying your body's physical reaction to emotional stimuli, take stock of how your breath is also affected (or keeping you from being affected). The following exercise is designed as an experiment to find emotional triggers using your breath. Using the concepts of depth, speed, inhalation, and exhalation, expand the experiment on your own. In class, I will often reference a, "doorway to emotion." Think of it like a decision you need to make, "Am I going to feel this, or am I going to contain it?" We are told so often to keep it together that actually feeling an emotion can be a difficult task. Use the questions at the bottom of the exercise to catalogue your experiences.

Instructions:

- Regulate your breath, inhaling through your nose and exhaling through your mouth.

- Deepen the breath and hold it in. Let it out quickly through your nose. Repeat several times. Tighten your shoulders, lock your knees, and try to move around the room with this breathing pattern.

- Breath in and out through your mouth quickly. Make the breath shallow. Tighten your hands into fists and clench your jaw.

- Repeat the last step, only alter your breathing, so it comes in and out through your nose.

- Breath in and out through your mouth slowly. Fill your lower back with a deep intake of air. After breathing this way for a few moments try to shake the breath on the way out. Kneel down in front of the chair. Place your head on your arms on the seat, continuing to breathe in this way. Try saying the word, "No," or, "Please."

- Breath in and out through your mouth quickly. Make the breath shallow. Smile. Bounce up and down on your toes. Shake your hands in front of your body quickly, as though shaking water off of them.

- Alter your breathing patterns. Feel free to add words or physical actions to help bring out authentic emotions. Use the following as a breathing guide:

  - Breathe out through the mouth or the nose
  - Breathe in through the mouth or the nose
  - Quicken the breath
  - Slow the breath
  - Deepen the breath
  - Make the breath shallow
  - Hold the breath
  - Shake the breath

Questions:

- How do you feel physically? Emotionally?

- Were you close to feeling an emotion? What stopped you? What helped?

- How much physical action do you need? How much do you rely on words to feel emotion?

There are many wonderful books on the subject of how to move the human body with dispatch and alacrity. However, reading will only get an actor so far. A diligent performer will train his/her body with private study, group classes, and master teachers. While looking for courses or exercises that will enhance your abilities on stage, always consider that connecting the body to intention and text is the ultimate goal. Below are some physical exercises that have helped me and my students.

Big Dog

(I credit Frank Deal with this exercise)

Props: A bone (anything from a shoe to an actual bone...). It should be small enough to "guard," but large enough to be a challenge for the little dogs. A quiet room is extremely helpful for this exercise.

Cast: Medium to large ensemble and a director

Time duration: Medium/variable (approximately 5 minutes for instructions and 3-5 minutes to play 1 round)

Overview: Without the power of speech, the ensemble will focus on the action of the "scene," while two (or more) of the ensemble engage in opposing objectives. The exercise develops listening, focus, imagination, intention, teamwork, and risk taking skills, with a primary focus on how the body is used.

Instructions:

• Seat the ensemble in a large circle

- Each actor will imagine a dog and demonstrate (individually) how that dog moves and sounds.

- Select one actor to be the "Big Dog."

- In the center of the circle, the Big Dog will be given a bone (the shoe) to guard. The Big Dog is not allowed to touch the bone during the exercise.

- Blindfold the Big Dog.

- All of the small dogs will bark and fill the room with noise. During the distraction, the director will pick one of the small dogs to attempt to steal the bone. Once the small dog acknowledges he/she has been selected, the director calls out, "Quiet in the yard!" At that point, the room should be silent again.

- Once it is quiet, Small Dog will attempt to steal the bone from the center of the circle and return it to his/her home without getting bitten by Big Dog.

- The Big Dog has three "bites" to protect the bone from the small dog(s) attempting to steal it. A bite is a point. It must be direct and specific (no waving the arm around). When the Big Dog bites, the director will call, "Hold." All action stops, and the director will call out how many bites the Big Dog has left, or the director will announce that the Small Dog has been bit. If Big Dog bites Small Dog, then Big Dog stays. If Small Dog returns the bone to his/her home, Small Dog becomes Big Dog.

- Some of the Big Dogs may have a gift for guarding their bones. If three rounds pass and the Big Dog catches every Small Dog who tries to steal the bone, make the game more challenging. Add another Small Dog and give the Big Dog five bites.

BODY EXERCISE 2
Isolation and Warmup

Props: An empty space with a mirror (optional) and room enough to lie down.

Cast: Individual

Time duration: Medium/variable (10 to 30 minutes)

Overview: Developing a body warmup is essential for maintaining the body's state of readiness. Most actors will have some sort of warmup before a performance; however, a good body warmup can be done each day, whether or not the actor is in performance or class. In this way, an actor has a neutral starting place to begin each day, and any additional body work he/she does is building off a firm foundation. The instructions below are a suggestion, and you are encouraged to build a warm up of your own based on the needs of your body. In addition to connecting movement with breath, the goal is the development of flexibility, strength, control, and intentionality of movement.

Instructions:

• Lay down on your back in a comfortable position, feet uncrossed, hands resting at your side, facing the ceiling.

• Inhale through your nose. Let your lower back fill up until it touches the floor (this may take some practice, so go as far as you can at first). At the same time, your stomach should also expand toward the ceiling.

• Exhale through your open mouth. The air should move at an unhindered pace (and it should be pretty warm). Push out all of the air left in your lungs and repeat the previous step. Continue deliberately breathing until your body is completely relaxed.

- Repeat this same breathing pattern while you move through the exercises. Inhale while tensing your various body parts; exhale when releasing tension.

- Point your toes toward the wall opposite your head. Release the tension. Do this five to ten times.

- Flex your feet so your toes point toward the ceiling. Release the tension. Do this five to ten times.

- Raise your right knee to your chest, engaging your quadricept. Release the tension. Alternating between right and left, do this five to ten times.

- With your feet out in front of you, legs fully extended, sit up and reach out for your toes, engaging your hamstrings. Do not bounce to get further; rather, do the stretch while inhaling, release the tension while exhaling, and inhale into a deeper stretch each time. If you can touch your toes without tension in your hamstrings, work toward grabbing your feet. If grabbing the feet doesn't work the muscle, lower your head to your knees.

- Lay back down on your back. Stretch your hands out, so they are perpendicular to your body (like you are showing your wingspan). Place your palms on the floor. While inhaling, rotate from the hips toward the right, raising your left shoulder off the ground. Alternating between right and left, release the tension and the breath. Do this five to ten times.

- Bring both knees up to your chest and hold them with your harms while inhaling. Your back should curve, and you should feel some good stretch in your lower back. Release the tension and the breath.

Do this five to ten times.

- Roll over on to your side. Draw your knees up to your chest in a fetal position.

- Roll over on to your front, with your knees below you. With arms outstretched, place your hands in front of you, palms facing down. This is the child's resting pose in yoga. Your arm sockets and lower back should enjoy a good stretch.

- Pull your feet under your body into a crouching position. Use your hands to push your legs straight.

- You should be bent at the hips, with your legs straight. While inhaling, straighten your spine, one vertebra at a time. Your head should come up last as though suspended by a string.

- Rotate your shoulders towards the front ten to fifteen times. Reverse the direction. Raise your shoulders as high as they will go with an inhale. With an exhale, release them.

- Draw your right arm across your chest, holding it in place with your left hand. Repeat with the left arm. Repeat five to ten times.

- Face the wall of the room and place your hands on the wall at shoulder height. Push off from the wall, gently. Bring your shoulders all the way to your hands and push off again, slowly (the slower, more deliberate, the better). Repeat five to ten times (keep breathing!).

- Face the center of the room again. Breathe in while making a tight fist. Release the fist and the breath at the same time. Do this same thing with each finger. Some fingers may be difficult to move without their neighbors moving as well. Do the best you can, and continually strive for more independent movement.

- Let your hand fall gently to the right. Breathe in and rest your right hand on your head. Do not pull your head down. Simply let the weight of your hand add some stretch. Release your head and your breath as you come back up to center. Repeat on the opposite side.

- In front of a mirror (optional) use your facial muscles to pull everything to the right. Pull down, left, and up. Repeat the exercise five to ten times and reverse the direction.

- Smile while only moving your mouth. Lower it. Raise your eyebrows. lower them.

- Hold your hands together in front of you. Don't interlock your fingers. Open your mouth, and let your jaw relax. Gently shake your arms back and forth, causing your jaw to flop open and shut. Vocalize while you do this by touching sound (see vocal exercises for touching sound).

Range Warmup

Props: An empty space with a mirror (optional) and room enough to lie down.

Cast: Individual

Time duration: Medium/variable (10 to 15 minutes)

Overview: Developing a vocal warmup is essential for maintaining the voice's state of readiness. Most actors will have some sort of warmup before a performance; however, a good vocal warmup can be done each day, whether or not the actor is in performance or class. In this way, an actor has a neutral starting place to begin each day, and any additional vocal work he/she does is building off a firm foundation. The instructions below are a suggestion, and you are encouraged to build a warm up of your own based on the needs of your voice. In addition to connecting strength, quality, and range with breath, the goal is the development the intentionality of sound. This exercise is based on Kristin Linklater's "touch of sound". Her book, Freeing the Natural Voice is a terrific resource for many other vocal exercises and theory.

Instructions:

- Lay down on your back with your hands at your sides. Raise your knees into a semi-supine position.

- Inhale through your nose. Let your lower back fill up until it touches the floor (this may take some practice, so go as far as you can at first). At the same time, your stomach should also expand toward the ceiling. It may help to rest your palms on your stomach in order to teach your core muscles where to engage.

- Exhale through your open mouth. The air should move at an un-hindered pace (and it should be pretty warm). Push out all of the air left in your lungs and repeat the previous step. Continue deliberately breathing until your body is completely relaxed.

- While exhaling, deliberately bring your vocal folds together with as little tension as possible. As soon as the folds come together, a low, soft sound is created, almost like a sigh (but far shorter in length). Just barely makes the sound and bring the vocal folds apart, letting the rest of the air escape. The sound is called phonating and should be the most relaxed sound you can make.

- As you develop skill making this sound, bounce of the sound two or three times as the air escapes.

- The pitch you are making is often quite lower than the pitch you use to speak. There are a number of reasons for this, but know that the voice created in this exercise is where your body makes sound with the least amount of tension. It is sometimes called your "true voice." Using the same pattern as before, bounce off the sound two or three times, and then sustain the sound on a hum. Simply close your mouth and let the phonation vibrate your lips until the air runs out.

- Repeat the same breathing/sound pattern, but as you progress, slur the pitch up above the starting pitch and back down below it, ever so slightly. Think of a mini siren. Gradually increase the range of the siren, making the highs higher, and the lows lower. Eventually, you will need to open your mouth to let the higher and lower sounds out.

- Do not push too hard in this exercise. If, at any time you feel tension in your neck, you need to stop. If the tension pursues, do not practice this exercise until a trained vocal coach has examined your technique and given you to go-ahead to continue.

Strength Warmup

Props: An empty space with a mirror (optional) and room to stretch.

Cast: Individual

Time duration: Medium/variable (10 to 30 minutes)

Overview: After completing Vocal Exercise #1: Range, it is now time to add power to the voice. Vocal power comes from three places: the breath, the resonators, and the intention. Be very aware of any strain or tension during the exercise. Remember to maintain the breathing techniques outlined in the body and voice exercises while working.

Instructions:

• Inhale through your nose. Let your lower back fill up at the same time your stomach is expanding outward. It may help to rest your palms on your stomach in order to teach your core muscles where to engage.

• Force the air out through your mouth on a "sh". Make sure the airflow is steady and the sound is loud. Push the air out until your lungs are empty. Repeat four to five times. Over time, your lung capacity and power will increase. This exercise is a marathon, not a sprint. Do the exercise without "end-gaming."

• Lay down on your back with your hands touching your cheeks and nose. Raise your knees into a semi-supine position. Touch sound, and try to increase the vibrations in your cheeks and nose. If you are having trouble increasing the vibrations, try the following:

– Close your mouth and hum
– Say "Nyah" or "Meanie"
– Say the "ng" sound

- Bring the sound into your chest. Place your hand on your chest to feel if the vibrations increase. In addition to imagining the sound lowering into your chest, play with pitch.

- Catalogue what sounds help resonate the chest area.

- Move the sound into the back of the head/neck. Place your hand behind your head, just below the "knot" in your skull. Open your mouth wide, and make the sound in the back of your mouth. This is a difficult resonator, and it will take time to make progress. Simply repeating the exercise will grow the skill. However, a private instructor may also offer insight if you are having problems.

- Using all of your resonators, say, "Ah-" Sustain this vowel and increase the strength by activating all of the resonators and increasing the amount and speed of the airflow. Aim the sound at an object a short distance away. Repeat this step to an object a medium distance away (10' or so). Repeat this step again to an object that is far away (30'-40' or so).

- Repeat the previous step using the following vowels: Oh, EE, OO, A

- Repeat the previous two steps with this change. Add a consonant in front of the vowel, and make the sounds in short bursts. Use the following consonants: F, V, B, P, D, T. When you are finished with the consonants, move into using "Hey." Vary tactics to change the intention.

BOUNDARIES EXERCISE

Part I

What an actor will or won't do in performance often comes from one of four different broad categories. Make a chart like the one below (give yourself some room to write in each box)

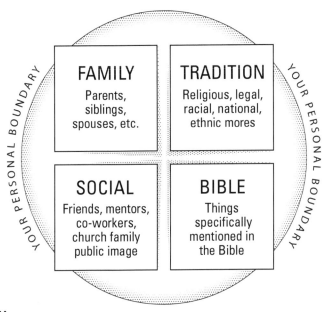

Part II

Make a list of the things that immediately come to mind that are currently boundaries for you (use the sample list as a starting place).

Sample Boundary List:

- Swearing
- Kissing
- Petting

- Violence
- Blasphemy
- Different Lifestyle

The broader the boundary (i.e. swearing), the more difficult it is to nail down. Make your boundary list specific to you. For example, instead of using swearing as a boundary, list the words you won't say.

Part III

Place each boundary in its appropriate quadrant. This is the most challenging part of the exercise. Be sure to deeply investigate each item on the list before assigning a category. If you think your family would have a problem with a list item, place that item in the "family" section. If you think your friends would be offended by anything on the list, place it in the "social" section. If you have any doubts at all about any of the items on the list...ask the people in whatever quadrant the item falls how they feel about you performing that specific action. Enlisting people from each category to either confirm or deny your boundaries will accomplish two things: They will know what page you are on (and vice-versa), and they will be aware of the types of moral questions with which you will eventually be faced. Lastly, you will finally have a good idea of why you are saying "no" to any given action.

Part IV

This list you create isn't static. It is intended to grow and change as you mature in your walk with God. Revisit this exercise throughout your career, letting the insights from your Bible study and counsel from other Christians inform your decisions.

End Notes

Chapter 1: The Parallels

1   Roberts, Kate Louise. *HOYT'S NEW CYCLOPEDIA OF PRACTICAL QUOTATIONS*, New York, Funk & Wagnalls Company, 1923, Print

2   Shakespeare.William, As You Like It, II.vii New Cambridge Shakespeare, 2012

3   Shakespeare.William, *A Midsummer Night's Dream*, III.i New Cambridge Shakespeare, 2003

4   Genesis 1:1-3, *The MacArthur Study Bible: New American Standard Bible*. Nashville: Nelson Bibles, 2006. Print.

5   Revelation 2:17, *The MacArthur Study Bible: New American Standard Bible*. Nashville: Nelson Bibles, 2006. Print.

6   Psalm 139:1-16, *The MacArthur Study Bible: New American Standard Bible*. Nashville: Nelson Bibles, 2006. Print.

7   John 17:6-12, *The MacArthur Study Bible: New American Standard Bible*. Nashville: Nelson Bibles, 2006. Print.

8   John 1:1, *The MacArthur Study Bible: New American Standard Bible*. Nashville: Nelson Bibles, 2006. Print.

9   John 17: 20-21, *The MacArthur Study Bible: New American Standard Bible*. Nashville: Nelson Bibles, 2006. Print.

10   Mark 10:35-40, *The MacArthur Study Bible: New American Standard Bible*. Nashville: Nelson Bibles, 2006. Print.

11   John 14:1-2, *The MacArthur Study Bible: New American Standard Bible*. Nashville: Nelson Bibles, 2006. Print.

12   John 16:13-14, *The MacArthur Study Bible: New American Standard Bible*. Nashville: Nelson Bibles, 2006. Print.

13   Bible Gateway. (n.d.) Notes John 16:7. Retrieved from https://www.biblegateway.com/passage/?search=john+16&version=NASB

14 John 16:13, *The MacArthur Study Bible: New American Standard Bible.* Nashville: Nelson Bibles, 2006. Print.

15 Romans 3:23, *The MacArthur Study Bible: New American Standard Bible.* Nashville: Nelson Bibles, 2006. Print.

16 Matthew 5:17, *The MacArthur Study Bible: New American Standard Bible.* Nashville: Nelson Bibles, 2006. Print.

Chapter 2: Empathy

1 Card, Orson S. *Ender's Game.* New York, NY: Tom Doherty Associates, LLC, 1991. Print.

2 Empathy. (2016) *In Oxford English Dictionary Online.* Retrieved from http://www.oed.com.lopes.idm.oclc.org/view/ Entry/61284?redirectedFrom=empathy#eid

3 Of course, there are always exceptions. If the actor is recreating Billy Holiday's performance, or is playing an historical character giving a famous speech, there are reasons for a touch of mimicry. The thought behind this section is to push the actor to create his own character, do his own work, rather than resting on the work of actors who have gone before.

4 *Little Shop of Horrors.* Dir. Frank Oz, Perf. Rick Moranis, Ellen Greene, Vincent Gardenia, Steve Martin, Warner Bros. 1986

5 Moore, Sonia. *The Stanislavski System*, The United States of America: Penguin, Print

6 Philippians 2:6-8, *The MacArthur Study Bible: New American Standard Bible.* Nashville: Nelson Bibles, 2006. Print.

7 John 12:47-49, *The MacArthur Study Bible: New American Standard Bible.* Nashville: Nelson Bibles, 2006. Print.

8 Romans 6:23, *The MacArthur Study Bible: New American Standard Bible.* Nashville: Nelson Bibles, 2006. Print.

9 John 3:16, *The MacArthur Study Bible: New American Standard Bible.* Nashville: Nelson Bibles, 2006. Print.

10   Luke 23:34, *The MacArthur Study Bible: New American Standard Bible*.
      Nashville: Nelson Bibles, 2006. Print.

11   Genesis, *The MacArthur Study Bible: New American Standard Bible*.
      Nashville: Nelson Bibles, 2006. Print.

12   This is by no means a comprehensive list. It is given as a springboard
      for actors who have trouble with the concept of the super objective.
      There are many things Jesus accomplished on the cross that satisfied
      basic human needs, and the Christian actor is encouraged to delve into
      those needs and apply them to his character work.

13   Shakespeare.William, *Hamlet, Prince of Denmark*, New Cambridge
      Shakespeare, 1994

14   Shakespeare.William, *Romeo and Juliet*, II.ii New Cambridge
      Shakespeare, 2012

15   Shakespeare.William, *Titus Andronicus*, III.i and IV.i New Cambridge
      Shakespeare, 2014

Chapter 3: Fear

1   *The Empire Strikes Back*. Dir. Irvin Kershner, Perf. Mark Hamill,
     Harrison Ford, Carrie Fisher, James Earl Jones, 20th Century Fox. 1980

2   "Iii. Anatomical Basis of the Memory Information System."
     Encyclopedia of the Human Brain. V.S. Ramachandran. Oxford: Elsevier
     Science & Technology, 2002. *Credo Reference*. Web. 31 May 2016.

3   1 John 4:4, 18, 16, *The MacArthur Study Bible: New American Standard
     Bible*. Nashville: Nelson Bibles, 2006. Print.

4   Keller, Timothy. "A Sickness Unto Death", Redeemer Presbyterian
     Church, New York, New York, Sept. 14, 2003, Sermon.

5   Matthew 17, *The MacArthur Study Bible: New American Standard Bible*.
     Nashville: Nelson Bibles, 2006. Print.

6   Esther 4:14b, *The MacArthur Study Bible: New American Standard Bible*.
     Nashville: Nelson Bibles, 2006. Print.

END NOTES

7   Judges 6, *The MacArthur Study Bible: New American Standard Bible.* Nashville: Nelson Bibles, 2006. Print.

8   A quick side note about being late. There are audition books out there that will tell you to lie when you are late. They advise the actor to say they had another audition that ran overtime. The books claim that a lie here accomplishes two things: the casting director will see the actor as "in demand," and the actor will have a legitimate sounding excuse. What the books do not address is what happens next. What should the answer be when the casting director asks, "Oh really? What was the audition for?" Or worse, "Who was casting the project?" My advice runs contrary to what most of the world has to say, probably because it comes from the Bible. Do not lie. Lies are the language of fear. Also, since there is no excuse for tardiness, do not offer one. It takes a great amount of courage (or a little bit of faith) to humble yourself and take responsibility.

9   Jeremiah 29:11, *The MacArthur Study Bible: New American Standard Bible.* Nashville: Nelson Bibles, 2006. Print.

10   Mark 10:35-45, *The MacArthur Study Bible: New American Standard Bible.* Nashville: Nelson Bibles, 2006. Print.

11   Secrets here refer to gossip and the like, not a character's secrets, which are actually quite useful when building a performance. What does your character know that the other characters don't? Is there anything your character knows that the audience is unaware of?

12   Shales, Tom, Miller, James Andrew. *Live From New York: An Uncensored History of Saturday Night Live,* U.S.A., Little, Brown and Company, 2002

13   These rules for improv can be found in schools, private studios, and all over the internet. Classes at Second City, The Groundlings, National Comedy Theatre, and Upright Citizens Brigade are all excellent places to go for training, whether you want to pursue a career in improv or you simply want to have some help conquering your fears.

14   Philippians 2:4, *The MacArthur Study Bible: New American Standard Bible.* Nashville: Nelson Bibles, 2006. Print.

15   Mark 12:30-31, *The MacArthur Study Bible: New American Standard Bible.* Nashville: Nelson Bibles, 2006. Print.

16   Isaiah 40, *The MacArthur Study Bible: New American Standard Bible.* Nashville: Nelson Bibles, 2006. Print.

17   2 Peter 3:9, *The MacArthur Study Bible: New American Standard Bible.* Nashville: Nelson Bibles, 2006. Print.

18   Daniel 4, *The MacArthur Study Bible: New American Standard Bible.* Nashville: Nelson Bibles, 2006. Print.

19   Psalm 90, *The MacArthur Study Bible: New American Standard Bible.* Nashville: Nelson Bibles, 2006. Print.

Chapter 4: Inspiration

1   QuotationsPage. (2015) Quotation details. Retrieved from http://www. quotationspage.com/quote/26135.html

2   *Raiders of the Lost Ark.* Dir. Steven Spielberg, Perf. Harrison Ford, Karen Allen, Paul Freeman, Paramount Pictures. 1981

3   2 Corinthians 12:9, *The MacArthur Study Bible: New American Standard Bible.* Nashville: Nelson Bibles, 2006. Print.

4   Lewis, C.S.. *Reflections on the Psalms.* Orlando: Harcourt, Inc., 1958, Print

5   Inspiration. (2016) *In Oxford English Dictionary Online.* Retrieved from http://www.oed.com.lopes.idm.oclc.org/view/ Entry/96980?redirectedFrom=inspiration#eid

6   2 Timothy 3:16, *The MacArthur Study Bible: New American Standard Bible.* Nashville: Nelson Bibles, 2006. Print.

7   Matthew 5:45, *The MacArthur Study Bible: New American Standard Bible.* Nashville: Nelson Bibles, 2006. Print.

8   Shaffer, Peter. *Amadeus.* New York: HarperColins, 2001, Print

9   Romans 1:20, *The MacArthur Study Bible: New American Standard Bible.* Nashville: Nelson Bibles, 2006. Print.

10   Moore, Sonia. *The Stanislavski System,* The United States of America: Penguin, Print

Chapter 5: Work Ethic

1   Adams, Douglas. *The Salmon of Doubt: Hitchhiking the Galaxy One Last Time*. New York. Balantine Books, 2002, Print

2   2 Thessalonians 3:10-12, *The MacArthur Study Bible: New American Standard Bible*. Nashville: Nelson Bibles, 2006. Print.

3   McMahon, Brendan. "Unemployment: A Lifestyle for Actors." Huffington Post, 4 Jan. 2012. Web. 30 May 2016

4   O'Neil, Brian. *Acting as a Business*. New York. First Vintage Books, 2009, Print

5   Colossians 3:23-24, *The MacArthur Study Bible: New American Standard Bible*. Nashville: Nelson Bibles, 2006. Print.

6   Moore, Sonia. *The Stanislavski System*, The United States of America: Penguin, Print

7   Proverbs 6, *The MacArthur Study Bible: New American Standard Bible*. Nashville: Nelson Bibles, 2006. Print.

8   *Minimum Salaries - Lort Agreement*. Agreements, actorsequity.org, (n.d.) http://www.actorsequity.org/agreements/agreement_info.asp?inc=031

9   Exodus 20, *The MacArthur Study Bible: New American Standard Bible*. Nashville: Nelson Bibles, 2006. Print.

Chapter 6: The Line: Strangers in a Strange Land

1   Chesterton, G.K.. *The Collected Works of G.K. Chesterton*. San Francisco, Ignatius Press, Print

2   Meatloaf. "I'd Do Anything for Love (But I Won't Do That)." *Bat out of Hell II: Back into Hell*. Jim Steinman, 1993 CD

3   John 17:17, *The MacArthur Study Bible: New American Standard Bible*. Nashville: Nelson Bibles, 2006. Print.

4   Matthew 5:17, *The MacArthur Study Bible: New American Standard Bible*. Nashville: Nelson Bibles, 2006. Print.

5   Romans 8:1, *The MacArthur Study Bible: New American Standard Bible*. Nashville: Nelson Bibles, 2006. Print.

6   John 8, *The MacArthur Study Bible: New American Standard Bible*. Nashville: Nelson Bibles, 2006. Print.

7   Matthew 5, *The MacArthur Study Bible: New American Standard Bible*. Nashville: Nelson Bibles, 2006. Print.

8   1 Corinthians 6:12, *The MacArthur Study Bible: New American Standard Bible*. Nashville: Nelson Bibles, 2006. Print.

9   1 Corinthians 10:23, *The MacArthur Study Bible: New American Standard Bible*. Nashville: Nelson Bibles, 2006. Print.

10 Romans 10:9-10, *The MacArthur Study Bible: New American Standard Bible*. Nashville: Nelson Bibles, 2006. Print.

11 Romans 6, *The MacArthur Study Bible: New American Standard Bible*. Nashville: Nelson Bibles, 2006. Print.

12 Matthew 6:33, *The MacArthur Study Bible: New American Standard Bible*. Nashville: Nelson Bibles, 2006. Print.

13 Isaiah 55:8, *The MacArthur Study Bible: New American Standard Bible*. Nashville: Nelson Bibles, 2006. Print.

14 James 4:17, *The MacArthur Study Bible: New American Standard Bible*. Nashville: Nelson Bibles, 2006. Print.

15 Lewis, C.S.. *The Silver Chair.* New York: HarperCollins, 1953, Print

16 Hosea 1:1-2, *The MacArthur Study Bible: New American Standard Bible*. Nashville: Nelson Bibles, 2006. Print.

17 Matthew 1:18-25, *The MacArthur Study Bible: New American Standard Bible*. Nashville: Nelson Bibles, 2006. Print.

18 Matthew 6:24, *The MacArthur Study Bible: New American Standard Bible*. Nashville: Nelson Bibles, 2006. Print.

19 Matthew 5:10-11, *The MacArthur Study Bible: New American Standard Bible*. Nashville: Nelson Bibles, 2006. Print.

Chapter 7: The Cost

1   Luke 14:28-33, *The MacArthur Study Bible: New American Standard Bible*. Nashville: Nelson Bibles, 2006. Print.

2   Psalm 139:14, *The MacArthur Study Bible: New American Standard Bible*. Nashville: Nelson Bibles, 2006. Print.

3   Jeremiah 29:11, *The MacArthur Study Bible: New American Standard Bible*. Nashville: Nelson Bibles, 2006. Print.

4   Brennan, Richard, Marwood, Stephen. *The Alexander Technique Manual*. Boston: Journey Editions, 1996, Print

5   Keller, Timothy. *The Reason for God: Belief in an Age of Skeptisism*. New York: Dutton, 2008, Print

6   Matthew 16:24-27, *The MacArthur Study Bible: New American Standard Bible*. Nashville: Nelson Bibles, 2006. Print.

7   Proverbs 8:17, *The MacArthur Study Bible: New American Standard Bible*. Nashville: Nelson Bibles, 2006. Print.

8   James 4:17, *The MacArthur Study Bible: New American Standard Bible*. Nashville: Nelson Bibles, 2006. Print.

9   Lewis, C.S.. *The Silver Chair*. New York: HarperCollins, 1953, Print

10   James 5:1-3, *The MacArthur Study Bible: New American Standard Bible*. Nashville: Nelson Bibles, 2006. Print.

11   Luke 19:10, *The MacArthur Study Bible: New American Standard Bible*. Nashville: Nelson Bibles, 2006. Print.

12   2 Peter 3:9, *The MacArthur Study Bible: New American Standard Bible*. Nashville: Nelson Bibles, 2006. Print.

13   This concept is laced throughout most of Timothy Keller's sermons and books. It is the backbone of his teaching, and in my opinion, why so many people are drawn to it.

14   1 John 4:4, *The MacArthur Study Bible: New American Standard Bible*. Nashville: Nelson Bibles, 2006. Print.

15   2 Corinthians 5:17 *The MacArthur Study Bible: New American Standard Bible*. Nashville: Nelson Bibles, 2006. Print.

Chapter 8: The Actor's Toolbox

1   2 Timothy 2:15, *The MacArthur Study Bible: New American Standard Bible*. Nashville: Nelson Bibles, 2006. Print.

2   Hitchens, Christopher. *God is Not Great*. New York: Twelve Hachette Book Group, 2007, Print

3   Genesis 27, *The MacArthur Study Bible: New American Standard Bible*. Nashville: Nelson Bibles, 2006. Print.

4   1 Samuel 16, *The MacArthur Study Bible: New American Standard Bible*. Nashville: Nelson Bibles, 2006. Print.

5   Genesis 37, *The MacArthur Study Bible: New American Standard Bible*. Nashville: Nelson Bibles, 2006. Print.

6   James 4:6, *The MacArthur Study Bible: New American Standard Bible*. Nashville: Nelson Bibles, 2006. Print.

7   John 20:24-28, *The MacArthur Study Bible: New American Standard Bible*. Nashville: Nelson Bibles, 2006. Print.

8   John 11:1-16, *The MacArthur Study Bible: New American Standard Bible*. Nashville: Nelson Bibles, 2006. Print.

9   John 14:4-6, *The MacArthur Study Bible: New American Standard Bible*. Nashville: Nelson Bibles, 2006. Print.

10   John 21:2, *The MacArthur Study Bible: New American Standard Bible*. Nashville: Nelson Bibles, 2006. Print.

Acknowledgements

This book was written over the last eight years,
and it would have stayed in my computer if not for
the contributions of the following people:

Karin Kary, my wife, and the first reader of every word I write.

Scott Campbell, my longtime friend and volunteer editor.

David Barker, Joshua Vanderpoel, Sam Varghese, and
Christine Marie McGinn, whose notes were invaluable.

Claude Pensis and Grand Canyon University, who gave me
an opportunity and a place to practice what I teach.

All of the actors who have passed through my classes
and challenged me on points theatrical and points theological.

My father, Ken Kary, who believed in me and what I had to say
enough to get these words on actual paper.